TELLING YOUR STORY

BOOKS BY *SAM KEEN*

GABRIEL MARCEL

APOLOGY FOR WONDER

TO A DANCING GOD

TELLING
YOUR STORY

*A Guide To Who You Are And
Who You Can Be*

Sam Keen and
Anne Valley Fox

DOUBLEDAY & COMPANY, INC.

GARDEN CITY, NEW YORK   1973

ISBN: 0-385-03046-0
Library of Congress Catalog Card Number 73-79636
Copyright © 1973 by Sam Keen and Anne Bartlett
First Edition

To the outlaws among us
who are living their own stories

Thank you to friends who shared stories with us, to strangers who entertained eavesdropping authors, and to Robert Poteete who cleaned up a lot of loose construction and dangling participles.

CONTENTS

TELLING YOUR STORY

I

TO TELL A STORY

Man is a storytelling animal. As our primitive ancestors sat around the fire carving spearheads and eating blackberries they told stories which in time were woven into a tapestry of myth and legend. These tales were the first encyclopedia of human knowledge. They explained where the world came from, why there were people, why snakes have no legs, why corn smut stops birth hemorrhages, why conch shells are sacred, why coyotes howl at night, and why the gods put fire and death on earth. In the dramatic telling the triumphs of heroes and the antics of fools came alive again. Stories told the people of a tribe who they were, where they had been, where they were going, and how to stay friendly with the spirits.

The myths of modern man are often unfocused; we don't celebrate our myths enough, they frequently hide like outlaws in the backwoods of the unconscious. For a variety of historical reasons (the emergence of machines, cities, anonymity, money, mass media, standardization, automation) we've lost awareness of storytelling as a way to dramatize and order human existence. But whether we acknowledge them or not, our myths and stories live in our imaginations.

To be a person is to have a story to tell. We become grounded in the present when we color in the outlines of the past and the future. Mythology can add perspective and excitement to your life. Within each of us there is a tribe with a complete cycle of legends and dances, songs to be sung. We were all born into rich mythical lives: we need only claim the stories that are our birthright.

With a little imagination each person can find within himself a replacement for the myths and stories lost when we ceased living in tribes. A person is a complex thing made up of a million individual smells, tastes, memories, and hopes. Listen for a few minutes to the voices that run through your mind. Every psyche is a private theater filled with scenes and characters. Listen and you will hear your father, mother, brothers, sisters, children, lovers, friends, enemies, teachers, and heroes seize your stage and act out their own dramas. Hear the multiple voices within yourself and you will remember that you belong to a special clan. Your people still inhabit you. They will help you to celebrate your myths, sing your songs, and tell your legends.

The techniques of storytelling and the psychology which underlies them rest on a discovery of the obvious: that what all persons have in common is their uniqueness. Every person has a story to tell. That's what makes a person. There are no autonomous, anonymous, pragmatic individuals. We were all raised by an intimate group that had traditions, values, rites of passage, ceremonies, and legends. We feel nameless and empty when we forget our stories, leave our heroes unsung, and ignore the rites that mark our passage from one stage of life into another.

We can rediscover the uniqueness of the person if we reassemble our myths and stories which have been homogenized into business, education, politics and dissipated in the media. Find the unconscious and make it conscious, find an audience for the untold tales, and you will discover you are already living a rich mythical life. What most of us lack is only the permission to tell the stories that are our own birthright.

You can't tell who you are unless someone is listening. There are better and easier ways to get an audience than by hiring a psychiatrist. Find a friend or lover to listen and tell your multiple stories, stories of your childhood, your family, your roots. Be all those characters who wander around in your head. Journey back into the past, ahead into your future, and out into cosmic time. Discover a few of your many selves.

The emphasis on telling stories amounts to a new way of defining personality and psychology. Psychology ought to be much more concerned with boredom and entertainment and much less concerned with mental illness and lost and found identity. The dis-ease of modern man's psyche is more of a vacuum than a thorn in the flesh. We are alienated, disgraced, frustrated, and bored because of what hasn't happened, because of potentialities we have not explored. Few of us know the fantastic characters, emotions, perceptions, and demons that inhabit the theaters that are our minds. We are encouraged to tell a single (true) story, construct a consistent character, fix an identity. We are thus defined more by neglected possibilities than by realized ones. We rehearse and repeat a monotonous monologue while heroes and villains, saints and madmen, ascetics and libertines wait in the wings for a chance to seize center stage and run wild. Identity is a repetition compulsion, a conspiracy to put a consistent face before the world, to cover up the glorious inconsistency of emotions and desires. The character we develop domesticates the world and leaves us no wilderness to play in. There are many territories of imagination and many strange regions of emotion that we may not enter without throwing our sanity into question. We remain rational, banal, boring, bored. A major concern of any therapeutic psychology should be to help an individual lose identity.

A psychological proposal is always political and this one proposes an ideal relationship between the individual and the community. Paradoxically, an individual becomes strongest, most vivid, and most open when he discovers the contradictions of his psyche. Each of us harbors the entire range of human possibilities. Every I is a we. We can become authentically public only by first going to the depths of the private. At the heart of the uniqueness of the individual lies the universal. Every person's deepest ecstasies and fears are old as mankind and common as dirt. Thus, the greatest freedom for the individual comes from the love of many stories. The strongest state is the one that keeps the fewest citizens in jails, insane asylums, and ghettos.

This book is designed to help you open the doors behind which you imprison the citizens of your private commonwealth. It is an invitation to form a community of teller and listener. It is a call to revolution; seize the authority to create your story.

II

THE KEY

Use this book as a travel guide. It provides theoretical maps (Philosophy), travel hints (Viewpoints), and firsthand accounts (Stories) to help you explore your own time, space, roots, and personal mythology.

The Philosophy that begins each section works as a large-scale map, a territorial overview. The broad theories of time and personality in these sections are pathways into experience. The maps chart known landmarks but leave many psychic frontiers uncharted.

The Viewpoints are designed to lead you on side trips to specific places within your mind and experience. They are like turnouts on a winding mountain road that let you see where you came from and where you are going.

The Stories (set off from the text by lines) are slides, souvenirs from personal journeys. We shaped and edited tales told to us by friends and by strangers on bus benches, as illustrations of the power of telling your own story.

It's your trip. Begin anywhere you want to—in the present, the past, the future, or in cosmic time. Do pass go! Move at your own speed. Get the lay of the land quickly, linger wherever you like the view. Mark spots of interest or mystery for later explorations. Enjoy moving or holding still.

The story is you.

III

THE PRESENT

It's a Long Way to
Here and Now

Intense pleasure sweeps time out of mind. In rare moments—
when the sun sinks into the sea, when thoughts couple to form
a metaphor, when lovers come together—all awareness focuses
on the here and now. When we are absorbed in thought or
action, consciousness advances gracefully along the retreating
edge of the present moment and we feel spontaneous and integrated.

Most people visit the state of pure awareness and ecstasy
from time to time but few can live there for long. Total concentration is as rare as it is precious. Our attention usually
is split. We take mind trips into the past or the future or retreat into fog. Or we jump out of our bodies and watch ourselves with others' eyes. And watch ourselves being watched.

In modern America the rush toward the here and now has
spawned a host of philosophical and psychological schools and

disciplines. Gestalt therapy works to clear away past and future fantasies that inhibit full involvement in the present moment. Transactional Analysis encourages the substitution of intimacy for game playing. Zen quiets the mind and teaches the art of eating, sleeping, and walking. Encounter and sensory awareness training aims at immediate expression of feelings and sensations. Psychedelics promise to open "the doors of perception" (Huxley) which lead to the Eternal Now.

In spite of the rhetoric of pure awareness and spontaneity, most of these movements understand that there is more to being in the present moment than letting go and flowing down the river. Awareness is only as profound as the person who is aware. We learn to see and feel profoundly as we integrate all that we have been and hope to be into the present moment. The most dynamic personalities are fully present in this moment without severing either memories of the past or visions of the future.

Boredom is imprisonment in one time and place. There are four human time zones in which we can travel. We can respond to the present, remember the past, anticipate the future, or stand in wonder in the eternity of cosmic time. Cultivate the ability to be in any of these zones and the here and now will be enriched with imports from other times and places. Travelers in time and space discover stories enough for a lifetime of entertainment.

THE PUBLIC SELF

Every person is composed of at least three nations—one public, one private, and one unknown. Each nation has its own boundaries, customs, laws, language, and traditions. Some boundaries are guarded and may be crossed only by trusted friends. The frontier between the known and the unknown self is always heavily guarded. No one of us can travel freely in the hidden places of his consciousness but, fortunately, messengers slip past the border guards and bring us dreams and images from the unknown. Ideally the highways that connect the nations should be well marked so that we can travel anywhere. But ignorance or fear keeps us from exploring the outer limits of ourselves.

Let's begin with the public self, the psychic territory that is supposed to be open to all—officials, acquaintances, colleagues, and strangers. The human animal is always social; there is no solitary self, no man is an island. Even when we retreat to solitude we carry within us myriad voices. When there's no one else to talk to we talk to ourselves.

The public self performs for an audience, real or fancied. It is the creation of the eyes that watch it. We learn to put on masks and costumes and play the roles society expects of us. A girl begins to learn what is expected of a woman the day her mother gives her a doll instead of an Erector set. Bankers shine their wing-tips, railroad engineers climb into overalls. Members of the counterculture identify each other by Volkswagens, knapsacks, overalls. By compounded example we learn the language and dress that are appropriate to our class and profession. But by changing your metaphors and images of yourself and your language, you can enlarge your public self and the possibilities open to you.

Most of us hate to admit that we conform to the dictates of groupthink. But clearly the need for social approval is as fundamental to the human animal as the need for food. Community is not a luxury for human beings. The self is created by its multiple presentations; without an audience there's no individual. So long as we do not identify totally with any single role—wife, lover, student, father, belly dancer—we remain free to explore the many possibilities of the private self as well as of the public self.

VIEWPOINTS

One way to identify your public self is to locate the words you most often use to describe yourself to others. The story of your official public self is told by the way you fill in blanks on insurance or tax questionnaires (name, age, sex, birthplace, marital status, police record, health, organizational affiliations). A more complex story is told by the terms you use to describe yourself to others.

> * Make a list of the ten words or phrases that describe you best. I am ———. They might be functions, feelings, activities, affiliations (ticket taker, frightened, Rotary Club president, student, competent, clown).
> * Stop. If you want to do the above, do it before reading further. Many of the Viewpoints introduce perspectives from which you can spy on yourself. The element of surprise may startle you into unfamiliar positions from which you can see what you've hidden from yourself.
> * Now rank the words or phrases in order of importance.
> * Now cross them out (give them up) one at a time until you are left with your single most important characteristic. By relinquishing your self-definitions one at a time you will get an idea of the most prized and the least crucial levels of your public self. (With two or more playing, this can be a revealing game.)

You are both like and unlike other persons. Only you can write your autobiography. But when it is written it will be a human story. If pride depends upon the sense of uniqueness, then humility rests upon awareness of our membership in humanity.

  * In what ways are you unique? What qualities distinguish you from your friends, your enemies, the masses? Do you think other people consider you unusual? Odd? Average? A character? An individual? Unobtrusive? Hostile? Do you agree with them?
  * If you were placed suddenly in an alien culture how would you identify with and distinguish yourself from the natives?
  * If you were to die tomorrow how much of the story of your life could be reconstructed from what other people know of you? Who knows you best? How much of your essential self is public and how much is private? How would you be remembered?

Somebody Meets Everyman

Unique? You bet I am! Haven't I spent most of my life proving it? Look around me, the stamp of my presence is everywhere. When I was eleven I learned about birds and gave my first lecture on ornithology to the local women's sewing circle: they thought I was wonderful, no other kid in town could do that! Another high moment was when I nearly flunked out of school while I was busy becoming the youngest Eagle Scout in the history of Maryland. All along, no matter what the crowd did I did the opposite. If they wore tuxedos I would show up in Levis. I made myself intriguing by being controversial and inaccessible. I sharpened my mind against the hardest ideas and largest men around. I climbed to the top of my profession so that I knew all the best people in my field in the country, and they knew me.

But then, by God, I found out it was lonely on that mountain top. All my will power scared people off; sure I was admired, but who enjoyed me? When my father died I realized that no uniqueness in the world could save me from ending up just like everyone else. The other day I saw an idiot in a coffeehouse laughing and moaning hysterically, on and on, completely out of control, and I thought, *what a curiosity he is,* and turned away from him. But underneath I knew that the only difference between him and me was that I keep my sense of absurdity under tight control and he lets his right out—he doesn't bother to pretend.

These days I do a lot more laughing and crying, and it's a great relief. I feel more of everything. My body gives me away: it hurts, it feels good, it demands to be fed, it needs to be touched. In the end it's the common things that actually make the difference.

THE PRIVATE SELF

The boundary between public and private is hard to distinguish. Privacy is always a matter of degree. At times we allow friends, lovers, family, or a stranger on an airplane to come behind the façade of our public images, but we often remain on stage even in intimate situations. Breadwinning husbands and housekeeping wives, for instance, can easily slip into allowing traditional sexual roles to inhibit their real desires, so that their public selves operate in the private sphere too. In this situation the deepest dimensions of privacy are experienced in isolation: the private self may be a locked inner room labeled NO ADMISSION.

Secrets come in all sizes and shapes, from adultery to xenophobia, but they cluster around the emotional centers of shame and elation. Many of the things we feel, desire, or do seem too shameful to be shared. We hide from public view fear, guilt, despair, impotence, cruelty, self-hatred, ugliness, and coldness of heart. We are afraid to let anyone see our degrading self-images, but we also conceal our tender ideals, grandiose visions, and ecstasies.

VIEWPOINTS

Sometimes you can dispel shame or expand pleasure by sharing your secrets.

* What are the secrets that you never (or rarely) share with anyone?
* What secrets would you be relieved to share? With whom? What will become of them, once told?
* Which are easier to share—the secrets of your idealized self or those of your degraded self?

Degraded self-images revolve around feelings of fear, weakness, anger, and confusion.

* In fantasy, allow yourself to be as weak, inadequate, passive, and ineffectual as you have ever feared yourself to be. Remember the times when you have felt small and helpless.
* Imagine that you are uncontrollably angry. Describe the persons you would punish, torture, or kill; the things you would destroy.
* If you lost your reason, your inhibiting forces, what form would your madness take?

Idealized images of the self usually cluster around fantasies of love, power, perfection, beauty, fame, knowledge, or creativity.

* Create a fantasy in which you become the fulfillment of your ideal self. You are strong, loving, beautiful, brilliant,

etc. What do you do with your power? What gives you the most pleasure?

* Chart the way you bounce back and forth between idealized and degraded images and feelings about yourself, between Infant and Superman, Earth Mother and Temptress, Master Builder and Caspar Milquetoast.

My Heart Was Clear as the Summer Sky

My life is full of secrets, all because I've done so many things and always had so much trouble with men. I'm outspoken by nature, but around the trailer court I try to keep my mouth shut about most things, because the older folks get offended by what I say. They don't much care for the plain truth.

My heart was clear as the summer sky until I lost Mick. We were married at eighteen and stayed passionately in love for eight years. Can you believe it? Then one night I was playing pinochle like I always did when Mick was working late, and I had the feeling that there was a ghost in the room. I kept looking up and around and swishing the air with my hand and then later they came in and told me he'd just been electrocuted in the mine, my Mick was dead. It must have happened fast because there was a great big grin on his face, but it wasn't so easy for me. All my hair fell out from grief.

I have a habit of falling in love. But ever since I lost Mick I fall *out* fast too—one good cry will do it. I've had a lot of experiences that I don't talk about much, mostly because people don't believe them, they get uncomfortable and shut right up. My longest secret is probably about Charlie. He was my boss when I was widowed in Oregon, and after a long time I got pregnant by him. He loved me but he couldn't marry me because he already had a family, so I real quick married some-

one else. Once when my son was five or six I ran into Charlie
in a restaurant in Seattle. He got very drunk and told my son
that he had three daughters and a half son whose mother he
would always love in his heart. When my son was eighteen I
told him that his father was someone long gone, but nobody
else ever knew. Even my husband thought that he fathered
that kid.

After a dozen stormy years with my second husband we
split up and I moved north. I opened a restaurant on the
Canadian border which really brought in the money, but then
I got hooked up with Harold, a good-looking fellow with the
charm of a rattlesnake, and that man tricked me out of half a
million dollars! Harold chased pretty girls and misused me, so
finally I let him go. After that divorce I decided that what I
really needed was to get me a man who carried a lunch pail.

So I found Oley and stopped running around with the
wealthy set and moved out of my beautiful house on the hill
to come here and live quietly. Oley's just about the sweetest
person I ever met except that he's got this drinking problem
and doesn't admit it so I have to cover up for him all the time.
Oley's problem makes one more secret in my life, that and
the fact that he and I aren't married the way we say we are.
Making it legal again just doesn't seem like a good idea. We've
been together for a few years and maybe it'll last, but you can
never be sure.

The thing I secretly wish is that Mick and I could have
stuck together all the way through, but death doesn't make
allowance for happiness. You go from lover to lover and place
to place and after a while you start getting confused. Things
don't stick together the way they used to, it's hard to tell
what's what. And in the end there's nobody that really knows
you.

THE UNKNOWN SELF

Consciousness is like a lantern on a dark night illuminating everything within a circle. When it's carried from one place to another some new obscurity surrounds the circle of clarity. What we know about ourselves is in continual dialogue with darkness. Self-knowledge and ignorance are linked because of the selective structure of the human mind. In focusing attention on one thing we ignore another.

The unknown self contains all of those experiences, feelings, fantasies, and possibilities that we repress rather than act out. This unconscious life erupts in dreams, slips of the tongue, projections of anger and love. What we don't know *does* hurt us, and help us.

Happiness is free flow between your known and unknown selves, trust in the compatibility of conscious and unconscious. The more we venture into the psychic depths the more likely we are to discover that the unknown is not peopled with enemies.

VIEWPOINTS

The known and the unknown are in constant dialogue. Look at one and you will get a reflection of the other.

* In an earlier Viewpoint you listed ten words and phrases that characterized you. Now make a list of ten characteristics you do *not* have—qualities, functions, feelings, or roles you find it important to deny. What characterizations would you strongly deny if they were applied to you (dull, manipulative, weakling, homosexual, gentle, introverted)?

* Stop. If you want to catch your unknown self off guard do the above before reading further.

One of Freud's basic rules for understanding the unconscious is that a negation is as good as an affirmation. What you strive to deny defines you as much as what you affirm. One way to explore the unknown self is to turn everything upside down. Assume that you are what you aren't and that you aren't what you are. Flip your story.

* Take your list of negations and compose convincing arguments to prove that these are your most essential qualities.
* Now take your earlier list of ten affirmations and show that these qualities do *not* characterize you. The most important and the least important qualities are to be reversed.

Another trick for stalking the unknown self is to picture your parents' psychological undergrounds. The fears, forbidden possibilities, and inconceivable alternatives of one generation are passed on in unspoken form to the next. Verbal preachments are not a part of the psychological underground: if you remember your mother saying, "A nice little girl doesn't stand on her head with a dress on," that is not an aspect of your unknown self. The non-verbal messages were transmitted in unconscious ways and are usually messages that your parents would deny having sent. Ask your ultramasculine father if he taught you that women are frightening enemies to be conquered and kept at a distance and he will likely deny it. Ask your anxious mother if she taught you never to be satisfied and she won't know where you got such an idea. Nevertheless, the messages were sent and received, in actions if not in words.

* What horrified your parents? What made them scold you?

* What topics of conversation were forbidden? How did
you know they were?
* What ways of life or habits were out of the question?
* What do you think your father and mother never did?

___

The Devil's Chariot

I am not: worrisome, inaccessible, romantic, idealistic,
addicted to dope, manipulative, a performer, inarticulate,
inattentive, or silly.

Or am I? I can take it easy with the best of them, but
somewhere under my blithe spirit I do worry a lot about losing
my center, being too open, getting closed down due to over-
exposure. There are a lot of mysterious things in myself that
I don't want to give to people, hidden places which I only
let a few chosen people see. . . . I'm really much less ac-
cessible than I pretend to be. But my romantic ideal, the self-
portrait I carry around in my mind, has no tolerance for
inaccessibility. The perfect me is always open to people and
information. When I'm feeling really high I do take a lot in,
but every so often that ideal gives way. Then I accuse
myself of being narrow and stunted, of blocking out the
world. . . . I guess that's where dope comes in. I'm addicted
to being high, cruising at my own speed. People often criti-
cize me for chasing highs, but I hate to feel hassled or
crowded and marijuana is a nice tranquilizer. It helps me
slow down and draw life in. It shuts out all those race-track
mind-trips where everybody leaves the starting gate at once
instead of just letting the horse gallop on his own time. . . .
I'm also pretty manipulative. I have a way of pretending to
let things happen when actually I'm making them happen the
way I want them to. It's like memorizing a recipe, filling the
cupboard, and then pretending to cook by feel—a little of

this, a little of that, and presto! A perfect pie! . . . That's
tied into being a performer. As a musician (and otherwise) I
use all the tricks I can to pull off the response I need from a
person or a group. It goes with my need to be smooth, to do
things with style. I pull off a lot of good performances, but
they're less spontaneous than they seem because of my need
to come off well. . . . I also have a way of speeding ahead or
jumping backward and missing what's happening right in
front of me, especially where words are concerned. I think I'm
articulate, but it takes so much energy to translate and hang
onto words that often I just withdraw, leave my body sitting
there, and turn inward. When I come back I find myself in
the center of a conversation with somebody stranded on the
other end. . . . Okay, yeah, I'm silly too sometimes. I act
that way in order to slip out of awkward situations. It hurts
to think of myself as silly. It's like dumb-blondeness, a misfire,
throwing away all your experience. I dislike myself when I'm
too stupid to see what I'm doing.

The other night all my negatives ganged up on me. I'd
been doing a lot of things for weeks without admitting that
they were hurting me, but they were. I dragged my guitar
and a pint of tequila to a friend's house downtown across
from a mortuary. I was wailing blues out the window, trying
to drown my depression in music, but this time it didn't
work. I sank lower and lower, still denying the stupid things
I was doing to myself. So finally I got in my car, rolled up
the windows, turned on the radio, and sped along the freeway
at seventy miles an hour. No one could come in, my defenses
were safe in my steel cocoon. I felt so sick I could hardly drive.
The freeway signs would read "next exit ¼ mile" and then it
would not appear. It was terrible, thrashing around on all that
hard concrete, whizzing right past bushes and grass and sky
on the Devil's Chariot. I didn't want to stop to look at the

dead thing that was trying to be born in me. I was using the freeway like a whip, trying to make a fast getaway: fill my head with noise, jump in my Chevy (the antithetical horse), and ride off to nowhere forever! It was stupid. As soon as I stopped I knew it. That's when I turned around, went to a friend's house, and cried my way back to a more natural, positive place.

BODYMIND

Our language, like a practiced magician, tricks us into believing in the existence of two separate entities called mind and body. Mindbody language reflects a persistent schizophrenic experience of the self, a dualism present in most civilized cultures. In Greek experience it was reflected in the dichotomy between soul and body, in Christianity in the warfare between spirit and flesh, in Victorian society in the tension between reason and emotion. We currently find it in the professional separation of physical and psychological medicine. It also occurs in the romantic idea that a person can superimpose a civilized mind dedicated to the virtues of work, reason, and control on a free, sensual body.

If we were fully integrated persons we might refer to ourselves as *being* bodyminds rather than as *having* bodies. We bring our whole selves—complete with autobiography—to every act of thinking or sensing. Eyes, ears, noses, mouths, genitals, and brains are all affected by history and politics.

The split between our bodies and our minds has a certain conservative survival value: so long as we *have* bodies we can deal with them as if they were possessions that we can manipulate or machines that can be repaired by experts when they break down.

It's comforting to believe that something (mind, soul, spirit) survives the death of the body. But to be fully thoughtful and sensuous is to be fully mortal. Death and sensuality belong together. Either/or dichotomies split us off from the erotic possibilities of personal integration. Mental and sensory awakenings are in no way mutually exclusive. If coming to our senses means losing our minds, it's a questionable trade. Brains and toes and belly are all erogenous zones, and who wants to lose one of those? The trick is to learn to be fully present in the world.

VIEWPOINTS

* Take a large piece of paper and an assortment of colored pencils or crayons and draw a picture of yourself in any way you want. It might be symbolic or literal, clothed or nude, a portrait or a full figure.
* Stop. If you plan to take this trip, do the above before reading further.

You are a body in a given time and place. The way you experience your body reflects your view of existence. Assume that the paper on which you just drew yourself is the world. What does your body-image tell you about your world?

* Do you fill all or part of your space?
* How realistic or symbolic is your representation of yourself?
* Is your outline sharp, fuzzy, disconnected, flowing?
* Is your figure open or closed?
* What parts of your body are missing? Out of proportion? Hidden?
* Are you clothed or nude? Is your body designed to be seen? Touched?
* What colors predominate?

* Give your drawing a name. What mythical (fairy tale, movie, television, storybook) character does it bring to mind?

It's not easy to keep track of all the parts of your body. There usually is a difference between what you think you feel and what you actually feel. Create a feeling map of the lively and sluggish areas of your body. Lie quietly in a comfortable position and focus your attention on your toes, insteps, ankles, and on up on all sides until you have traveled over your entire body.

* Where do you feel numb, tense, warm, electric, heavy, constricted, relaxed?
* When you locate a part of your body that is numb or hurting, take a trip inside, try to find out why. See if there's anything you can do to relax it or make it feel better.

DRAW HERE

FRIENDLY EYES OR DEADLY WATCHERS

The eyes have it. We are lookers. Of the many possible ways of knowing, we prefer the mode that lets us watch, keeps us spectators. From a distance it's easier to observe, to discern forms and patterns, and to categorize. When we neglect our other senses it is hard to imagine what it might be like to perceive the world through smell, taste, sound, or touch. By definition, we can't see what it would be like to feel any other way.

The eyes may be used to observe or to caress, to keep a safe distance or to pull things closer to us. When the eyes dominate, the more intimate senses may be neglected. Instead of touching we examine, judge. We become spectators, passive, distant from the world, watchers not responsible for what occurs. Then our passivity makes us victims rather than initiators.

Self-consciousness and paranoia are the results of hyperobjectivity and self-criticism. In self-consciousness the I watches rather than acts. In paranoia the eyes are projected onto an enemy—"they are watching me."

The spectator stance is rooted in childhood. In infancy we were watched over. The omniscient eyes of parents bathed us in smiles (maybe) and fended off hot stoves, barking dogs, and strangers. But the caring eyes also were prying, seeing around and through us. We were secure but transparent. In time we wanted freedom enough to dare secrecy. In hideaways under weeping willows, or behind cellar doors, we gained self-knowledge and shame. When we played I'll-show-you-mine-if-you-will-show-me-yours we found that self-consciousness shadows the steps of each new freedom.

But the judging eyes were not easily escaped. The watch-dogs of social morality warned us that God could see where parents could not, and conscience (the internalized eyes) reminded us when we were doing anything bad, mad, or dangerous. Thus, conscience made watchers of us all. For most of us, growing up meant transferring the authority from parental and divine eyes to those of society—teachers, bosses, mates, review boards, neighbors, and police. The eyes were everywhere.

Pure spontaneity—freedom from all watchers—is rare, but it is possible to mitigate self-consciousness. One good way to begin is by recovering the use of our other senses. Once we remove from our eyes and brains the pressure to control, the other senses are free to receive.

VIEWPOINTS

Eyes can do many things. They may be hard or soft, focused or unfocused, penetrating or caressing, dull or sparkling, darting or open. Change the eye that sees and you change the world that is seen. What is the relationship between your feelings about the world and the way you use your eyes?

* Open and close your eyes for several minutes. Each time you close them tighten and squeeze your eye muscles. When you open your eyes, relax. Continue until you feel your vision blur and soften. Notice how your peripheral vision increases as sharpness of focus decreases. What happens to your other senses when you see the world through a soft haze?

* When you are in a public place, watch eyes. Observe the stories being told by challenging looks, furtive glances, intense concentration. Notice where eyes focus and where

they don't. Where are public eyes forbidden to linger? (Try staring at someone's sausage in a restaurant!)

Indentifying the eyes you imagine are watching and judging you is one way to move beyond self-consciousness to greater spontaneity.

* When were you first aware of being watched?
* Who is watching you now?
* For what imagined audience do you perform? Dress? Work? Create? Make love?
* What look is most often in the eyes of your watchers? Do your actions please them or do they disapprove? Of what are you proud or ashamed when you imagine that X is watching you?
* When you are most self-conscious and self-critical what ideal are you chasing?
* If you weren't busy watching yourself, what would you do?

The Trouble with Maraschino Cherries

As a kid I was sure that my father saw every move I made. Even though he apparently had only two eyes, he always seemed to catch my slightest slip-up. One day he lined up his five children in the kitchen and demanded a confession from the one who ate the maraschino cherries. I said I didn't do it, but then he made us stick out our tongues and, sure enough, there was mine pink as a third-degree burn. He spanked me twice that time: once for lying and once for snitching the cherries.

I learned to outfox my father by doing most of my trespassing outside the house. But then I discovered God, and was trapped again. God had some really rigid puritanical ideas like, "Whosoever looks at a woman with lust in his

heart has sinned . . ." and, since I figured that went for
girls too, I was worried. It was no longer good enough to
hide or minimize my weaknesses: now I had to be pure to the
core. God was probably nowhere around, but His witnesses
tricked me into the habit of watching myself with the eyes of
a slavemaster!

By the time I was sixteen and sexy I was looking up to my
older sister instead of Jesus. I thought she was wild and
beautiful and brave, and I wanted to be like her but didn't
quite dare. God and my father were still casting their little
shadows over me, frowning at my excesses. So I was stuck in
limbo. I had the feeling that my sister also was watching me
now, and over and over again I imagined her disappointment
at my cowardice. For years I carried her around in my mind
like a tiny Buddha, sitting in the corner silently watching,
appearing and disappearing. When I married before I was
really ready she seemed disappointed and distant. When I
chased after random good graces she seemed to be laughing
at me. Whenever I backed myself into a sharp corner she
pointed to an opposite possibility and I felt torn in two.

Then, gradually, I learned the amazing truth: I am my own
worst watcher. Half the time I watch myself like a cool, distant audience checking for grace, humor, passion, accuracy,
and spontaneity in every action! Other times I jump behind
the eyes of someone specific—waitress, cab driver, enemy—
and look over at myself the way the others used to do. These
watchers are always equipped with stern and perfect vision.
If I see them seeing me acting foolish or vulnerable in any way
I feel suddenly appalled, and withdraw from whatever's
happening. Those sickening moments I leave my friends (over
there with *her,* acting like asses!) in the lurch.

More than anything else in the world I want to learn to
feel myself from the inside rather than *watch* myself from

the outside with that mean set of eyes. Lately I've had some new experiences of absolute self-acceptance: suddenly I am my own best friend and anything I do or feel is all right. Eye strain and migraines dissolve, and I feel euphoric toward everything around me. It's like discovering an air pocket in a hurricane.

SEX: WHAT EVERYBODY KNOWS

Sex, sex, sex.

A plethora of words, ideas, theories, pictures, and opinions about how it ought to be; experts on every corner telling us how to achieve better orgasms and perfectly liberated relationships; the promise in advertising and pornography that sex is as simple, natural, and easy as hello and good-by; our own conversational assertions that our sex lives are beautiful.

So why is sex such an obsession with us? If it's all happening slam bam thank you ma'am with everyone coming two at a time whenever we please, why is it so much on our minds?

Birds and bees do it naturally by the numbers and the seasons, but it seems that human beings have always invented meanings for sex. Because we are cultural animals we interpret, symbolize, and mythologize the major biological acts of existence—birth, death, sex, eating, excreting, sleeping. Long ago we defined masculinity and femininity by social and economic roles and agreed to live accordingly.

But our social and sexual contracts are changing. The sexual revolution now under way is based on a radical questioning of traditional Western ideas of womanhood, manhood, motherhood, and the institution of marriage as the officially sanctioned place for sexual meeting. With those old certainties suspended we now have the chance to define ourselves in new ways.

Since sex is so important to us, and since the old sexual-social assumptions are being questioned, and since we all have bodies, each person can come up with a sexual style that is harmonious with what he wants out of life as a whole. It's a major task, but it can be a delightful one. Without absolute rights or wrongs, the guideline is the pursuit of what is satisfying and fitting for your life.

Trust your body.

Do what feels good.

VIEWPOINTS

Traditionally, masculine and feminine characteristics and virtues have been juxtaposed:

FEMININE	MASCULINE
passive	active, aggressive
soft	hard
nurturing	protecting
patient	insistent
welcoming	penetrating
oriented toward the private sphere of home, family, and children	oriented toward the public sphere of politics, and war
symbolized by the left hand, darkness, the moon	symbolized by the right hand, light, the sun
governed by emotion, hence mysterious and dangerous	governed by reason, hence responsible
submissive	dominant
inferior	superior

* How much has your self-image been shaped by these stereotyped notions and roles?
* Tell the story of how you learned what a woman or man was supposed to want and be.
* How satisfied or frustrated are you with the current standards of sexuality? With your own sexuality?
* If you could change places with your mate or lover, what would be the easiest and hardest aspects of your new roles? What changes would you make in your relationship?

Your body contains both male and female hormones just as your psyche includes developed images of the ideal male and female. By looking at men and women you admire and desire, masculine and feminine figures in your dreams, you will get an idea of your own sexual archetypes.

* How do you experience the masculine characteristics and feminine characteristics in yourself?
* Develop a dialogue between the man and the woman within you. Let them talk to each other. How does the feminine side of your personality relate to the masculine side? How does the man in you want to be loved by the woman?
* Take yourself on a fantasy trip in which your masculine and feminine parts are all sexually satisfied.

Try some new sexual languages. Experiment with changing the words you use. What happens?

Myths are frequently created to explain why there are two sexes and a variety of sexual preference. In Genesis, Eve was liberated from Adam's rib so that man could have a companion. Plato said that people were once joined back to back —woman-woman, man-man, man-woman, until finally the gods took compassion and split them down the middle so they could face each other and make love.

Make up your own myth about the origin of sexes. Or redesign them altogether (try a world with one sex, or four).

The Invisible Home Run

When I was twelve I wanted to be a boy in the worst way. I played great baseball and dreamed of joining the school team but I knew they'd never let me, so I put on a T-shirt to show my flat chest and applied for bat boy. One afternoon they let me do it but then the girls came and pulled my cap off and my hair fell down and everyone laughed. That was the end of that.

In the eighth grade I was crazy to be a sports announcer since I couldn't play professionally myself. I painted stripes on a beer bottle, turned it upside down, and announced all the plays from the top of the bleachers. I was obsessed. But one day it hit me that the whole dream was futile—the world would never accept me as a sports announcer—so after everyone left the field I went down, slugged an invisible home run, jogged around the bases, and walked slowly home. At that moment I lost all interest in baseball and haven't watched a single game since. . . .

At seventeen I still didn't have any breasts—not the slightest sign of them. All my boy friends turned out to be friends. I practiced kissing the bathroom mirror and saying "yes," but nothing happened. I was sure that God was punishing me for shunning my femininity for so long. Finally my mother took me to a doctor who gave me some hormone shots and a few long weeks later I was profusely bleeding and budding. I was hugely relieved, but still I felt like a fake for needing so much help just to become a woman.

*   *

By now it's clear to me that nobody's got it made. The feminine personality feels to me essentially sturdy, self-aware, remorseful, dependent, confused, frivolous, self-deprecating, emotional, and bored. Men are generally blockish, competitive, hostile, arrogant, aggressive, emotionally bottled, articulate, and vulnerable. The male stance essentially says, "I am what I am," while the female sends a lot of double messages (just look at our eyes, flashing like berserk runway flags—one eye dropping a tear and the other painted for seduction!). But in order to support their artificial superiority men have to be constantly equipped to do battle, and they end up lying to themselves a lot to disguise the tender feelings which get in the way. At the core I feel mostly feminine and soft and proud but sometimes I wish I had more courage. On the other hand, their physiology makes men vulnerable in a way that women aren't. When the penis goes limp at the wrong time (and who's got remote control?) a man gets wiped out. The same thing happens to women, of course, but it's not so obvious. Women are able to keep up two faces, but at the same time we get stagnant and bored because we're not *forced* to act in the outside world.

*   *

If I'd been born a man I'm sure I'd have twice the amount of money, job status, and worldly confidence that I have now. Of course I'd also lose my easy access to men with power (they take you places for show, or make love to you as if you were a goddess) but it would be worth it. I'd be a human being and people (men especially) would listen to me, respect me, maybe even like me for once! As a man I hope I'd be confident enough to enjoy women—especially strong ones—and not fall into treating them like dumb passive playthings.

Sexually, the major change in my behavior would concern

seductions. Most men have no idea what power there is in gentleness: they handle footballs and hammers more sensitively than a human body. As a man (probably in love with a woman like me!) I could afford to be a deeply attentive lover, since I'd know that women castrate when they feel cheated or overlooked, not because they are natural-born bitches.

TIME FRAMES *Where Is Now?*

What's happening? What's going on now? Where in the world are we? If only we could hook up a meta-computer to an omniscient sensing device we could, in theory, create a machine that would give us an accurate read-out on the exact placement of every particle in the universe at this precise moment. And then we would know what's happening at this point in time.

But this moment and the meaning of this moment—fact and interpretation—are not separable. Human beings inevitably are philosophical animals. We interpret, discover, and create meaning in the act of perception. We think with our senses, see with our hearts, and feel with our brains. We use images, analogies, and metaphors to understand the world around us and the meaning of life as a whole. We live within a framework that gives meaning to our experience. The philosophical context within which we live determines the way we perceive the content of our days. G. K. Chesterton had a sense of this when he advised landlords to inquire after a potential tenant's philosophy of life rather than his financial affairs. A man who constantly feels the pressure of time running out just might run out himself.

The history of religion and philosophy provides a handy exhibit of images and analogies that can be used to frame experience. Each world view embodies a philosophy of time that gives meaning to the present moment. What's happening always depends on a myth or metaphor that explains why anything is happening:

If the world is an artifact shaped by a divine craftsman (Plato), then time is the moving image of eternity and this moment should be used for contemplating the eternal forms and making things in the world conform to them.

If the world is a battleground on which the forces of evil have nearly defeated the forces of goodness (Gnosticism, Manicheanism), then time is a prison that keeps man's spirit locked into matter and this moment should be used for escape.

If the world is a material illusion in an eternal sea of nothingness (Buddhism), then time is a dream and this moment is for enlightenment, awakening from illusion.

If the world is the arena God has assigned to His free creatures (Christianity), then time is an opportunity for freedom and the present moment may be used for deciding, creating, and enjoying.

If the world is a happenstance conjunction of erratic atoms (atheistic existentialism), then time is unbridled chaos and it doesn't matter what you do with the present moment.

If the world is a mystery to be savored, and used responsibly but never explained, then time is the filter through which the human animal perceives the mystery of being, and now is a strange gift that will never come again.

If the world is an immense organism that is always dying and being reborn like a plant (cosmic, maternal religions, Nietzsche), then time is a recurring cycle and this moment is not new and may occur again and again.

If the world is a place where only the fit survive (evolutionary capitalism), then time is money and this moment should be used productively to better oneself in the competition . . .

Many of us have no such systematic philosophies in which to frame our understanding of time so we make do with more modest images, intuitions, or feelings. Time is an old gypsy, or a snake that swallows its own tail. It is for killing or filling, using or keeping track of, or improving. When we suspect that time is running down (the golden ages are all in the past; glory is gone with childhood) we face our accumulating years with dread of decay. In more buoyant moments when time seems to be moving toward fulfillment (the New Jerusalem, or maturity), we feel the years mellowing us like fine wine. However modest or elaborate our principles of interpretation are, they will be homogenized into the way we experience this passing moment.

VIEWPOINTS

Your time shows your limits. Whether you believe in reincarnation or the finality of death, in cyclical or linear time, this moment is in the context of a larger picture. Draw a life-map, a diagram, a chart, or a time-line that will point to where you are now.

* How much time have you spent? How much is left?
* Do you like the way you've spent your time so far?
* Have you been here before? Will you be here again?
* Where are you going? Where have you come from?
* What is the meaning of time for you? Are you on the road to somewhere, do you want to be going, is where you are now all right with you?

DRAW HERE

An Imaginary Line

I started out drawing my life-map in good spirits and ended up feeling foul: instead of picturing a meandering road or an open space bubbled with galaxies or something fluid, I turn out a regular progress graph! It's that damn straight line down the center that holds me accountable, always judging me in terms of how high I leap or how low I sink. And to make it worse, so few of the jags ever really get off the ground. . . .

I suppose my high/low graphing system got set up way back when I was a kid. I was a skinny little guy with red hair and slow-motion responses and an older sister who grabbed up all the attention. My childhood wasn't particularly traumatic, it was just low on *triumphs:* it's as if I walked around in continual low-level anxiety, all the time hugging an imaginary line. Things that happened infrequently, or experiences that were too good or too spooky to believe, just didn't register with me, which is probably why so much subtlety and richness got left off my map.

In college things picked up some, but then I joined the Marines and disengaged again. For three years my body went through active maneuvers while my mind stayed aloof. I ruminated a lot, chewing the cud of past experiences, and refused to accept what was going on around me as very real or relevant. I was a Marine fighting in Vietnam but it hardly registered; even now it's hard to believe I was there. My Lais probably happen that way: people just don't bother to *be there* and so they don't make distinctions between shooting at targets and shooting at soldiers, between shooting at people and shooting at babies.

After graduate school I got really excited about my work, which then shot me into an even higher wave of political activism. At the peak of all that I fell in love and was feeling really fantastic, but I guess I wasn't going to escape the straight line that easily. . . . All of a sudden there was a tragedy on the other side of the country and my marriage celebration was postponed and everything caved in at once, like a parachute hitting ground. After that I hobbled along the old line for a long time, feeling generally anxious and negative. It's only recently—since my move to another town— that I finally seem to be getting recharged.

As a matter of fact, my graph does show something new happening. Instead of a median line chewed up by little saw teeth it looks like I'm beginning to ride rhythmic waves: high energy and excitement at the crest, low energy and relaxation in the trough. When I look at my life that way I don't have to box it up or kill the past off with retrospective judgments. If my life's a wave, then there's no pass or fail, just the building and falling and building. That means I don't have to invent a superman to live up to or a nebish to live down.

So right now I'm sliding down the back of a six-month high into a low pocket, getting ready to digest and ruminate before starting up a new front of excitation or risk-taking of some sort. If this last hill represents a trend, then my wave-curves are definitely getting smoother and the space between them is lengthening, all of which is reflected in the fact that my feelings are thawing out. Hopefully this mellowing process will continue so that the wave amplitude peaks when I'm about fifty, stays high for a while, and then very gradually tapers down until at some point I just stop living. I'm not young enough any more to be interested in those sharp roller-

coaster curves where every day's a whole new goddamn turning point. But I do look forward to deepening involvements
and periodic rest and nice smooth wave-sets rolling into the
future.

THE PAST

It's Still Happening

We are the Now Generation. We love the present tense. Be here *now*. Yesterday is gone and best forgotten; our tradition is to have no tradition. We aren't Europeans buried in ancient tombs and cathedrals and medieval ruins. We were born yesterday and we will be young forever. Over thirty is over the bridge. Age embarrasses us; remembrance is a function of senility. We exile the aged to Sun City leper colonies so they won't impair our illusion of endless summer.

But history's not so easily dismissed. Repressed memories, national or personal, won't stay down. To be alive is to have a past. Our only choice is whether we will repress or re-create the past. Childhood may be distant, but it is never quite lost; as full-grown men and women we carry tiny laughing and whimpering children around inside us. We either repress the past and continue to fight its wars with new personnel or we invite it into awareness so that we may see how it has shaped the present.

The moment you begin to tell your stories you may find that memory is a trickster who picks and chooses scenes. What happened to you in the past has yet to be determined. Ninety-nine times you tell the story of the day you were whipped for stealing apples you didn't steal. Then, in the hundredth telling, you remember that you *did* steal them and the whole scene changes. Your memories of what happened to you in 1953 will be different in 1975, and again in 1984.

Both national histories and individual autobiographies are passional accounts of the past. They are not a collection of objective facts but stories constructed to prove some point. History is more like myth than science in that it justifies some present custom or value.

The past is open to revision because memory is a function of present intention. History is always constructed to prove some point. If you were a poor abused child, a victim of parents and circumstances, you probably will continue to be a victim. If as a child you chose your responses to people and surroundings you probably will continue to be a free agent. You probably will discover in your future about as much freedom as you can find in your past.

The following pages suggest ways that you can turn your story over (and over) and find new perspectives on past events and emotions. You may invent a new past and open up a novel future.

CLAN AND FAMILY

Every person is plural. There is no *I* without *we*. Each of us was shaped by a social group. To know yourself is to understand your people. There is no psychology without sociology.

Every family has rules, customs, mores, traditions, taboos, rituals, and habitual ways of interacting that shape and shade the personality of each member. Your individual story is set within a framework of family history.

VIEWPOINTS

Who are you? Where did you come from? Who are your people? Detail stimulates memory. By recapturing specific events and scenes from your past, you can trace a thread of detail from the known into the unknown. Reconstruct the physical setting of your childhood and you may recover the flavor of the family in which your psyche was first marinated.

* Draw a detailed floor plan of a house you lived in before you were ten.
* As you enter each room imagine the furniture, pictures, smells, and events you associate with the room.
* Where were your secret places? (Where did you stash your comic books or go when you wanted to be alone?)
* Who lived in the house with you?
* What was the dominant mood in the household?
* Which rooms are you unable to reconstruct in memory? Why do you think you forgot them?
* Are there rooms you can't enter?

After you've filled in as much detail as you can remember, take someone on a tour of your house. Describe it as a novelist would so that your listener can feel the texture of the couch you lay on when you were sick, smell the bread baking, feel the emotions that permeated the house.

If you are playing with these Viewpoints in a group, use

several persons to create a living sculpture of your family. Or pose your family members in an imaginary photograph that would represent their relative positions.

* What position did each member occupy?
* Are your parents facing each other, going in opposite directions, on the same level? Are they supportive or antagonistic? Who is leaning on whom?
* Which members are close to each other and which are distant? Where is the center of the family?
* What are the basic bonds and jealousies among the siblings?
* Who is trying to get away from the family?

DRAW HERE

The Palace

I lived with my mother, father, and little brother in the same house for twenty years. The others are still there. The rooms are always filled with fresh-cut flowers and colorful paintings. The furniture is tasteful and the house is handsome, but underneath it something is uneasy. I think I grew up in its image.

As long as I can remember, my mother's been queen of the palace. This should have made royalty of the rest of us but it didn't work that way. Mother shuffled us like face cards in a marked deck. To live in the house we signed a contract to play by her rules.

I think of the house in four sections. My room, Daniel's room, and Dad's study are outposts surrounding the kitchen. Daniel spends most of his life upstairs in his room with electric trains and microscopes and scrap metal. Dad's desk sits in a nook behind the staircase downstairs. Although no one will admit it, the den is rarely used for anything but storage, so Dad can sit there undisturbed, paying his bills.

My room is on the bottom floor at the end of a long cold hallway, cavelike, but full of its own sunshine. It was my sanctuary, and I felt uneasy when the others came down there. Mom and Dad owned the walls, but I plastered them over, inch by inch, with photographs and lovely paintings (mine)—pictures from my imagination. The bookshelves were another barricade against my parents and their world. Neither of them read much, so the books symbolized my separateness.

On winter afternoons Dan and I used to sit at the dining-room table with our homework. The dining room opens into the kitchen where Mother was inevitably puttering and keeping a protective eye on us. The kitchen was her special kingdom: the refrigerator a treasure chest, the sink a well, the TV a music box.

Dinnertime was crucial. Everyone had to be presentable and prompt. The whole thing is unpleasant to think about mostly because at Mom's dinner table I felt like a second-class citizen. Dad always said his piece first: what happened at the office, family decisions to be made, et cetera. Then there would be some political argument, arrogant bullshit all around, me struggling to overpower Dad, hoping to prove my first-class status. But Mom protected him. She set him up as head of the royal family, although we all knew it was she who really ruled.

My parents' bedroom is the only room I left out of the drawing. It falls off the left edge of the page. I guess that's because it's their exclusive territory, the place where they make love and plot together. What that area of the house meant to me was a full-length mirror and a heated bathroom. I used the mirror when no one was around, but the bathroom was a constant sore spot. Mother used it as a power tool, jealously guarding the hot water in case Dad should suddenly want a shower in the middle of the afternoon! My basement bathroom was cold and uncomfortable but theirs was taboo for me unless Dad was out of town.

Mom has always guarded Dad's space. They married when Mom and I escaped from wartime Germany. I was five then. I think maybe her protectiveness toward him was a compensation for her fierce attachment to me: I was all that was left of her family. Anyhow, she trained me (and later Daniel) not to talk back to our father. She said that she could "take it and bear it" but that he "deserved respect"—which made him seem ridiculously fragile.

So the queen was also the sacrificial lamb. Mom always let us know what motherhood cost her in dollars and pain, and

we felt appropriately guilty. I began to see the price I paid
to live in that privileged kingdom. In exchange for being a
good girl (finishing college, looking lovely, holding down jobs
I didn't like, vacationing with the family) I received money
and food and praise. But always I had to explain *why* I
wanted something, which translated into: "What did you do
to deserve it?" and "You can't always have what you want."
Simply saying "I want" was never quite good enough.

I lived in that lovely house like a lady in waiting until I left
to find out what else I might be. Mom keeps my bedroom
filled with fresh flowers, but until I know more about what
I want for my own life, it doesn't make any sense to go home
again.

TRIBES

Pre-modern peoples didn't think of themselves as individuals
—they were members of a tribe as well as of a family. Ancient philosophers knew that human dignity begins with "We
are a people, therefore I am." Modern people are tribal too
but we call our tribes by different names—churches, corporations, states, nations. Each of us was nurtured within and
shaped by several corporate bodies, voluntary organizations
and professional corporations that molded our values and
behavior—schools, sororities, businesses, clubs, temples, bowling teams, local, national, international governments.

VIEWPOINTS

Those organizations in which we learn and work absorb the
major part of the time we spend away from families. Schools

and businesses create an important part of the mythology of our clan: "Education is the key to success."

* Draw floor plans of your earliest schoolrooms. Which of Mrs. Brace's litanies still clutter your mind? ("Raise your hand before speaking." "Set the example, don't *be* the example.") How did you feel on the first and last days of school? What values did you learn along with arithmetic? Citizenship? Good conduct? Respect for authority?

And, "Financial success is the foundation of lasting happiness."

* What did you first get paid to do?
* What part has work played in your life? Is it different from play? What do you value more? How valuable would you be without it?

We move in and out of groups and organizations. Each corporate body has its way of defining membership. Construct a collage from the symbols of your loyalties.

* What uniforms or emblems have you worn? (Scout? Drum and Bugle Corps? Army?)
* What pledges have you taken, what creeds affirmed? (On my honor I will . . ." "I believe in . . .") How many do you still honor? Did you honor them at the time?
* What secret initiations have you undergone and what was your reward?

National allegiance is the modern equivalent of tribal loyalty. Patriotism is the magic of transferring familial feelings (Fatherland, Motherland) to a political entity. This trick is accomplished by creating a national history which all citizens share. The younger generation is initiated into the stories that The People (Zulus, Americans, Cubans) have always told.

* What does it mean to you to have English, Irish, Polish, German blood?
* What are your distinguishing national characteristics? What stories and jokes taught you that the Irish brawl, Jews make money, French make love, Mexicans are lazy, Americans are foolish, other stereotypes?

Bitterly Hoeing and Mowing

God knows how I loathe free time, so whenever He wants to punish me He makes me stop working. I manage to avoid manufactured three-day week ends and personal vacations, but legal holidays are inescapable. Even if I go to the office as usual there's no one around to hand me manuscripts or respond to my memos or bring me coffee. I usually end up going to some damn office party which only exacerbates my frustration.

A good workday is something I can feel the instant I wake up in the morning. If I'm not abnormally depressed or hung over my fingers and toes start wiggling and right away my head's popping with great ideas. During breakfast I chew on plans and memos and then rush to the office. On the best days everything goes smoothly into gear with me at the wheel.

I haven't always loved my work. As a kid I spent half my life bitterly hoeing and mowing. We had a hopeless lawn, cows, and no fence, and my mother had a way of making everything doubly unpleasant. It was a lousy lawn, a lousy house, a lousy life. Once I tried to throw over the whole thing, permanently. I got appendicitis and ate a box of epsom salts and spent my sixteenth birthday in the hospital trying to die.

My father was a skilled plumber and mechanic. I worked

in his garage for twelve years. Then I went away to college and learned, in a freshman physics course, how a combustion engine is put together. My father knew a lot, but he never taught me any of it. He was such a good craftsman that he must have had some joy or pride in him, but even that he managed to keep hidden.

Before I became an editor I was a reporter for a large newspaper. I didn't have any of the money or status or authority that I have now, but I felt self-righteous just the same because I was working so hard. Newspaper work meant daily pressure and steady teamwork. I loved the intensity. I think it was during those years that I established myself as out of sync with mankind: I had Wednesdays and Thursdays off, so I escaped those horrid week ends that drove other people into society.

If I were suddenly forced to retire, I'd probably kill myself. When I'm working I'm potent and important. It's not the same any place else in my life. I often envy my kids because they don't work and don't seem to need to, but I'm too far gone for that. Besides, there's always the danger that if I stopped driving myself I'd find how nice it feels and never work again. . . . I'd end up running off to Acapulco and receding into lower-middle-class penury, and then God would spite me and I'd be mowing lawns again!

A life of leisure is out of the question. I only know how to relax under the pressure and concentration of hard work. When I lose myself in problem-solving I feel (for a short time) powerful and collected. As long as the world's workload holds out, I'm sure I'll go on working like a maniac, placating God, and resenting my children. After all, I do all that so terribly well. . . .

Walking to Work

I figure that a person's work is whatever he does best. For me, that's walking. Twenty-two years ago, when I was forty, I dropped out and slowed down and never checked in again. I live off a small veteran's pension. Every morning I wake up early, walk down the hill to town, and start strolling. I look at things and think about things and say hello and good-by to whomever I happen to pass. Sometimes I go to the post office to check my box and stare at the mail, or to the bakery for a cup of coffee. Often I sit for several hours on the bus bench, watching traffic and feeling the sun on me. In between I just walk.

It took me years to learn how to do this well. At first I was always interrupting myself, asking guilty questions like: what are you producing? what do you do for other people? One thing I'm sure of, I'm not doing anyone any harm. Most people spend their days making cookies and doorknobs and weapons. I feel my body swinging down the street and know I'm doing at least as much as those people do. Anyway, with over half the output in America wasted on war and defense, I'm glad to be a non-contributor. . . .

So my job is walking down the street celebrating the existence of things. Someone's got to do it! This is a small town and a lot of people probably think I'm crazy—Harvard graduate wandering around like the town bum for twenty years— but I don't care. I'm too busy appreciating the clouds and trees and sounds that most people rush right past. These things need to be celebrated, so how can I stop to worry about what I'm *not* doing?

Every night when I go to sleep I die, and every morning I'm born again. I walk and see and "emanate"—as Robert Graves would say. All the time I'm thinking and watching myself grow fuller and lighter over the years. It's a fine life's work; I'm good at it, and there's no retirement in sight.

THE GEOGRAPHY OF THE PSYCHE

We can't separate who we are from where we are. People are rooted in time and place, so our psychic space is generously seasoned with memories of physical territories. The Montana-born may feel claustrophobic in city streets that seem spacious to New Yorkers. The geography of our past is part of memory.

The link between turf and psyche is the result of early associations. When you were a child there probably were places you could and couldn't go. We learned to connect busy streets and the yards of cranky neighbors with the dangerous unknown. Later the same taboos were extended to tattoo parlors, whorehouses, and neighborhoods on the other side of the tracks. Every human emotion is seeded in the sights, smells, sounds, and tastes of specific environments.

It is possible to explore the geography of your psyche by reconstructing the places where you have lived. Start with the smell of a pizza parlor and it might lead you back to your first date. Conversely, emotions can be traced backward to specific places: panic may be connected with the image of being smothered under blankets or being lost in the woods; happiness may be a milk shake at the corner drugstore; freedom may be jetting through the night in the back seat of a 1941 Ford.

VIEWPOINTS

Re-create with words or drawings the childhood environment
you remember best. Concentrate on the city or countryside
that lay beyond the intimate space you occupied with your
family.

* Take an imaginary walk through your home town and
see what people, places, smells, and feelings pop up.
* What places were taboo? Where *didn't* you go?
* What social, regional, political, class, and economic pe-
culiarities of your environment seasoned your early life?
* What aspects of your early locales are still real, important to you? Which have you moved away from?

The Fishnet

When we moved to Southern California from the East
Coast I was deeply impressed by four things: the wide, sandy
beaches; the mass of cars (especially forest-green Porsches)
on the road; people walking around half naked; and the bold
pink paint job on my grammar school.

Our town was a neat middle-class suburb of Los Angeles,
caught up on three sides by multi-lane freeways and major
boulevards, circled by Hollywood and Beverly Hills, Culver
City used-car lots, huge aeronautics plants, the International
Airport, and the dusty old downtown area a dozen miles east.
During my twelve years there I remember exactly two family
trips downtown: one to see *Flower Drum Song* at the Shriner
Auditorium and the other to order a pair of glasses from the
City Teachers' Optical Exchange. The town was like a fish
tangled in a huge net. Those of us who lived north of the

tracks coped with the existence of Los Angeles largely by ig-
noring it. We kept to ourselves, clinging to the sleek public
beaches on our western border.

Every sunny summer day we went to the beach and swam
and played volley ball and lay around on beach towels with
Cokes and candy bars and transistor radios. A couple of miles
south of lifeguard stand number 2 where our crowd gathered
was an old fishing pier that reeked of bait and fried fish and
cotton candy. The clientele was mostly senior citizens and
Muscle Beach queers, so any time we got bored we walked
down there for a freak show. In the late afternoons we strag-
gled home with the soles of our feet burned from asphalt and
hot sand, and smelling of salt water and Coppertone. My
girl friends and I stripped naked in front of the bathroom
mirror and compared our young bodies, all of them smooth
and brown and blonde.

The endless summers faded by late October. Winter days
were moderately cool with occasional rain or fog. I loved to
see the palm trees with their tops lopped off by sheets of fog,
and to smell the air stained with eucalyptus after a good rain.
But I didn't really pay much attention to trees. By the time
I was in high school the slick, bleached, one-dimensional
Southern California style seemed one hundred per cent normal to me. The laundromat, bowling alley, bakery dispensary,
cycle shop, crab-grass lawns, and taco stand dripping with
ground beef which I passed on my way to school were the
other half of the world to me. High school was made up of
oatmeal cookies, eraser crumbs, bus fumes, and dirty gym
clothes. What else was there?

It was only when I left town after graduation that I saw
what my town didn't have. Other parts of the country had
different attractions: winter, spring, and fall; clear air; street
theater and town meetings; farms and vegetable gardens;

witchcraft and new music. I saw how life in suburban Los Angeles had flattened me. I'd learned to be cool and flowing, but not to stand out or think creatively or go for broke.

So for a long time I was fascinated with anything ethnic or eccentric. At nineteen I remember listening to a Russian/ Jewish/American poet read her poems with such vigorous feeling that I sat in the audience and wept over my own lack of "heritage" or "character," resolving to flee to Georgia or southern France where I'd grow pecans or learn a language with soul!

Instead I went to San Francisco, Manhattan, Montana, and Washington, D.C., and even back to Los Angeles for a while to live downtown with "the people." Now I'm ready to settle somewhere, but the question is, where? I like fluidity and expanse (as in freeways and ocean) but I hate the predictable, mono-emotional nature of what I grew up in. I need color and sharp edges as well as roots. I need to belong to something I make for myself. But where is it? And what is it: a place? a work? a people? I've dropped pieces of myself all over the place, and now I want to gather some of them together.

The Wilderness Within

Beneath my urban exterior there are pine trees, sage grass, and redheaded woodpeckers.

I had an old-fashioned childhood, much more like Tom Sawyer's than Holden Caulfield's. My family moved every year or two from one small southern town to another. This meant that my brother and I were always outsiders, handy scapegoats for the established gangs. In rubber-gun and BB-gun wars we were the targets. But the moment we took to the woods we were foxes. We ran along invisible paths and lost our pursuers with ease and then circled around to laugh at their confusion. No one could trace us to our hidden lairs. I remember one fortress we made beneath a large fallen tree. We hollowed out a space and wove saplings together to form the sides and top and camouflaged the whole thing with fallen branches. It was so well hidden that it took us several tries before we could find it on the run. Occasionally some earnest scoutmaster would bring a troop of forty boys into our woods for tests in tracking and woodmanship. On those glorious days we changed trail markers, laid false trails, and stalked around creating unbelievable chaos. To this day I have dreams in which someone is chasing me in the woods, but for me these are delightful. I know I can pull out a trick or two and outwit my pursuers.

No matter where I am in the world I can feel the mud from the creek ooze up between my toes and the cool water from the swimming hole dripping off my body when I need to. My images of absolute harmony are of lying in the grass in the sun getting dry and warm and listening to the gurgling of the water, and of walking home in the dusk when a silver note of a wood thrush rises up to join the light of the first star. At the end of the day we were happy to be going home to a warm dinner and parents who were just as glad to see us returning as they had been to get rid of us that morning.

Words Never Worked

The eight of us—plus poor old Elizabeth McCarthy before she dropped dead in the attic room—lived in a huge beat-up asbestos house in small-town Massachusetts. The place was a wreck. Paint-chipped walls, stains, knobs missing from

doors, and that damp back room with the hanging light bulb
where we buried the winter's rubbers and ice skates and
sweaters—all reeking with mold. There were two garbage
cans in the front yard that marked our compound like twin
tombstones. They were crawling with maggots. Even now it
gives me the creeps to think of my mother's hands inspecting
us for worms.

It wasn't that we were destitute so much as that no one
much cared about keeping things together. Father worked
all day in a dye factory and couldn't cope very well when he
came home. He would wander around the house babbling in
incoherent Italian/New England/alcoholese. Mother nursed
at the mental hospital every night till midnight. The rest of
the family watched a lot of TV, generally avoiding one another.

Our gangly household was centered around one basic
taboo: no real conversation allowed. In a thousand unspoken
ways we were discouraged from saying anything substantial
to one another. Father waited up every night for Mother to
come home (he's probably there now, snoring in the maroon
chair, insulated by the TV) and as soon as she was in the door
they started up their noisy battles. Over and over they shouted
the same accusations, but since neither one ever listened you
couldn't really call it communication. Occasionally one of
them would slobber out an "I love you" or something to one
of us, but that didn't mean much either. Outside of our parents' cyclical hostilities there was just no room in our house
for emotional expressions.

There were, however, occasional moratoriums, days when
the cold war was dropped and we all talked and touched
each other. Christmas, Easter, and Thanksgiving were like
bright slides flashed on a blank screen. The constricting taboos

were set aside and we were generous and affectionate, even excessive (having saved up all year!) with one another. All of a sudden the eight of us shared a unified dream, even if it was only a belief in Santa Claus. It was fabulous. I remember how one Christmas Eve the priest announced that God was real but Santa wasn't. On the way home from mass Mom and Dad told us not to worry about it, that this time the Father was mistaken, and we gladly believed them. Holidays were rare occasions for me, times when I didn't have to worry about my tender feelings hanging out.

Two years ago Mother insisted, as she always does, that everyone come home for Thanksgiving dinner. I knew it was impossible, but for the hundredth time the desire to be at ease, to be part of a family that *talked* to one another got the best of me. We assembled, thirteen of us now, dead-ended around the living room, wondering what to say to one another, fighting the urge to switch on the television. Mother was in the kitchen completing the last details of dinner. Finally she brought it all out—turkey, cranberries, peas, onions, mashed potatoes, sweet potatoes, pickles, jellies, bread, pies, strong Irish coffee—and placed it, chilled and steaming, on the long table while the rest of us watched.

After she lifted her fork Mother excused herself, went upstairs, overdosed herself with barbiturates, and passed out. I found her draped on the bed and called an ambulance. At the hospital they pumped her stomach and tucked her in to sleep it off. Mother hadn't intended to die. She told me later she saw Father kissing a neighbor over the back fence and "just had to do something to change the rules." Words had never worked with them, so she gathered her most vulnerable audience and staged a statement of her anger, one which we all understood.

After the hospital phoned to say that Mother would be all right, the rest of us crept to the table and picked away at the cold feast in silence.

MORALS, MANNERS AND FOLK TALES

Culture is a machine for conserving, discovering, and sharing knowledge. Knowledge is conveyed by two processes: teaching and learning.

Teaching requires a formal situation in which there is a clear distinction between the informed and the ignorant. Before we are old enough to defend ourselves, parents, preachers, and teachers systematically teach us the myths, morals, and manners they believe we need to know in order to be civilized. But learning often takes place unconsciously and informally. Usually we learn best when we are enjoying ourselves most: songs, jokes, and stories told just for the fun of it worm their way into our imaginations and nibble at the core of our more serious beliefs.

The things we learn by ourselves—the knowledge we assimilated by osmosis when Dylan sang, "The times they are a-changing"—strike deeper than the lessons that were formally taught to us. We were taught that all men are equal in the eyes of God and the law, but in stereotyped stories and jokes we gathered that Polocks, niggers, queers, and stutterers were not quite right and not equal. We were taught that honesty is the best policy, but we saw that actually tact (lying), cleverness (cheating), and legal loopholes (stealing) were acceptable aids for getting along in the world. Official morals and myths are ideals, not actualities, and no culture wholly believes in its own propaganda. Thus, what we are taught comes to us tinged with conflict and ambivalence, and that's usually the way we pass it on.

VIEWPOINTS

Some of the tension and ambiguity you experienced within yourself may be a result of contradictory messages received as a child from parents and other adults. Because their ideals and their actualities were at war with each other, they may have said one thing and done another. They had enough cynicism and idealism to warn you: "Do as I say, not as I do," but while they instructed you in their hopes, their fears came alive for you too.

> * What ten commandments would best summarize the rules, ideals, and taboos your family advocated? (You shall earn your living and your dignity by work. You shall appear moderate, polite, and gentle no matter how you feel.)
> * What jokes, stories, and tales were told until they were polished as river-bed pebbles: what were the unconscious messages hidden within your family's oral tradition?
> * What feelings about sex did you get from "dirty" jokes and formal sex instruction?
> * Who were the good and bad, clean and dirty characters in your family lore? What jokes were told?

The Texas Ranger

When I was a boy Dad told me a story I never forgot. In the early forties, driving through Texas, he stopped at a diner where an old-timer asked him if he was driving toward Dallas. Dad said yes and invited the stranger to ride along.

As they drove through the long night the man began to tell stories about his days as a Texas Ranger. He told about the time he and another Ranger thought they had a killer trapped in a cabin. They called for him to come out and were answered by gunfire. They shot back. When the battle was over there were three dead men in the cabin, but it turned out that none of them was the suspect. As the stranger got out of the car in Dallas he said to my father, "I've seen a lot of things I wish I hadn't seen."

I think Dad told me this story as a kind of warning: watch what you do because the consequences of a false move will scar you for life. For years I respected this message. I was afraid of making irreparable mistakes because I didn't know about second and third chances. But finally I broke some rules and took some risks and buried my father, and the whole thing turned over. Now I think that what I'll regret most when I'm old is not anything I've seen or done but the things I was simply too timid to try.

RELICS AND TALISMANS

There are things that promise to outlast all of us. Bach is dead and his music is everywhere. One way mortals defy time is by investing themselves in durable things that can be passed from generation to generation. Such inherited objects are a mixed blessing. While we gain power from inheritance we are also defined and limited by it: we come trailing streams of karma and leading white elephants.

The things that one generation wills to another insure continuity. Cultures differ in their ideas of what possessions, rights, and obligations of the fathers should be visited upon the children. It may be land, titles, livestock, wives,

ceremonial equipment and religious rites, songs, personal clothing and body adornments, antiques, money, stocks and bonds.
All souvenirs are reminders of what has come before us. Part
of each person's life is recorded in the objects he leaves to his
survivors.

VIEWPOINTS

Legacies come in tangible and intangible forms.

* What heirlooms have you inherited? (Antiques? Jew-
elry? Clothing? Books? Property?)
* What objects of sentimental or personal significance do
you have that once belonged to someone else? (Conjuring
stones? A wedding ring? Lock of hair? Pictures?) Why do
you keep them?
* To what extent has inherited money shaped your life?
* What personal qualities were gifts from persons who are
no longer living? Whom are you living up to? Who died
for you?

Thinking about the residue that will remain after you die
is a good way to clarify the values in which you are now
investing your time and energy.

* Make an imaginary will in which you bequeath your personal and financial possessions. Note which things you
value most.
* What personal qualities would you like to assign to family and friends? Which do you hope to bury with you?

Driftwood and Love Letters

When Dad died my relic stock pile instantly doubled. He
owned little of economic value, few antiques, no land or
money. The things he loved were all sensory objects: Navajo

rugs, a turquoise belt buckle, a seventy-pound shell of a man-eating clam, pieces of driftwood he found and fondled, little medicine bottles full of polished stones or sea shells or copper pennies, and an old hickory walking stick with a fistlike gnarl at one end which he rubbed with oil and crushed wheat until it was perfectly cured. I chose these things to keep because they remind me of the special way my father had of touching things, of using his hands to relate to the world. From him I inherited a kind of permission to caress what is beautiful.

My mother and grandmother used to sew clothes for me. When I was thirteen they made me a brown cowboy shirt embroidered in beautiful greens and oranges. When I moved from Tennessee to Delaware the kids teased me for looking like Tex Ritter, so I hung the shirt up. But I've kept it all these years because my dreams of woods and animals and wide-open spaces are woven into it.

I keep my personal memorabilia in an artillery-shell trunk in a closet. It contains old diaries, newspaper clippings, snapshots, souvenirs from my trip out West at seventeen, my Eagle Scout badge, and love letters from all my old girl friends. There are also letters from my fifth-grade teacher, Miss Beech, who drew birds in pastels on the stationery and wrote that I was "tough as a tiger." I don't want all of this stuff directly around me, but I don't want to throw it away either. It's a way of preserving my past without actually having to lug it with me. The photographs are especially good that way. They whisper, *"You were there,"* about stages along my way, reminding me that I came from somewhere.

The Glass Box

My grandfather was a turn-of-the-century robber baron, a giant who took what he wanted. Anyone who owned an oil field within his reach had reason to worry. Grandfather came on like a tidal wave, crushing and liquidating everything in his path. He was a classic Oil King. My father inherited a furtune and at the age of thirty decided to sit it out: no work, no society, no real friends. Now he and my mother dole out huge hunks of money to me, like monthly dog biscuits. I guess that arrangement makes me *dependently* wealthy, but anyway I'm very rich. . . .

I was born in a gilded crib that was heavy as gold. For forty-one years I've been languishing in it like Scrooge in his money bins, and it's not likely to dry up. I'm attached to the things money buys. My clothes are simple but obviously expensive and tasteful; they make me a country gentleman. I love fast cars and schooners, and the power to arrive anywhere, any time. My money buys superior education and homes for me and my family. It also insures that we will never starve or go unattended. Grandfather's fortune sets me apart from other people.

But money inhibits too. At five I was the perfect little gentleman, perfectly polite, superior and stifled. My mother made a habit of pointing her finger at people who made fools of themselves, teaching me by negative example to avoid extremes. I was courteous, thoughtful, obedient, well mannered, and completely sheltered from all expressions of anger or ecstasy. Women without breeding were known to be lurking everywhere, hoping to cast a spell over me and my money.

So I lived like a rare orchid painted into a landscape, so protected from the hard, real-world experiences which define most people that I grew up smooth, without muscles or scars. While the other kids were out tearing around town on their paper routes I was in my glass box keeping clean. I remember the time my father gave me a Brownie box camera. I liked it a lot, so right away he bought me an expensive Leica, which killed the excitement. I felt overwhelmed and left out.

The real things I needed from my father he never offered. His single message about sex, for instance, was that if he ever caught me carrying contraceptives (and he would find out, he said, because they leave rings on wallet leather) he'd beat the hell out of me. I was fifteen, and that was the first and last word from him, but somehow I inherited his sexual timidities.

So I floated through college and the Army looking out of my glass box, but nothing got through to me. I took on some wives and children and hobbies but still avoided the world, living inside my own loneliness. I began to see myself as a pool of gelatin—not jello, which has a flavor—but an inert blob that does nothing.

I was so submerged in my legacy that up until a couple of years ago I had no idea what I desired. Finally, greatly depressed, I deduced that the elegant, timeless existence that money provides is not enough, that a person needs a work, a skill. I went back to school to earn a degree in film making.

My wife says that my "menopausal ambitions" to become a film maker are unrealistic. I'm banking on the hope that she's wrong. Reaching out like this is very painful, but by now it's do or die. I get terribly limp and despondent sometimes, but even in my worst depressions I never consider renouncing my fortune. It's too late for that, the prestige and security of having money holds me together like a cellophane skin. Even professional competency isn't likely to relieve that dependency, but I still have hopes of being acknowledged and useful to society, of pulling myself up from the gilded bed. I don't want to die of the old family disease. . . .

GIFTS AND WOUNDS

Everyone alive has received some share of the gifts that make and keep human life human. The giving and receiving of gifts plays a large part in most cultures. Gift giving is rooted in the primal feeling that the world itself is a gift, a banquet already spread before us when we arrive on the scene. Something—chance, God, the trickster, or divine reason—arranged things to support human life. The rains come, the corn grows, and the yearly harvest is followed by a thanksgiving festival. We give gifts because life is given to us. We can repress it or throw it away, but we can't hold onto it. Recent psychological tests suggest that the person most predisposed to develop cancer is the one who fails to express his emotions. Generosity is a recycling of the gifts of life.

Wounds are as universal as gifts: sooner or later suffering and death strike us all. The ancients wove myths around this basic ambiguity of life. Father Time (the Greek god Chronos) is the devourer of his children; Kali (the Hindu goddess of creativity) often appears with motherly arms and blood dripping from her lips.

In a famous case in American law Justice Holmes decided the suit of a blind man against a construction company for injuries received when the man fell into an open ditch. The ditch had been marked with smudge pots and signs but the blind man, who refused to use a cane or any other device to guide him, missed the warnings. Holmes argued that, since society is composed of persons who are all crippled and limited in some way, each person has the obligation to protect others from his own limitations. The blind man forfeited his right to damages when he transferred to others the responsibility for dealing with his affliction. Society is a brotherhood of the gifted and the wounded. As individuals we differ only in the composition of our assets and limitations.

That society is unjust often means that one man's gift is another man's wound. Scarsdale and Harlem, wealth and poverty, privilege and oppression co-exist in unholy symbiosis. But things are more than what they seem. Rich is better than hungry, but injustice may create a supportive community among victims while the exploiters suffer anomie. Anxiety and madness can be the price of creative genius. Gifts and wounds fit together like yang and yin.

VIEWPOINTS

Resentment, anger, and hostility are gauges of the real and imaginary injuries you have suffered.

* What persons, events, and institutions arouse your greatest resentment or anger? Who frustrated, neglected, manipulated, inhibited, or repressed you?
* In what ways have wounds made you stronger?

Gratitude is the expected response to a gift. But gifts may also trigger feelings of embarrassment, obligation, or confusion.

* What gifts have bound you to the giver, made you dependent, weaker? Did you realize it at the time, or only later?
* When have you been singled out for special attention? What persons have enriched your life by caring, teaching, challenging, delighting in you?
* Flip your story. Make a convincing argument that your

gifts are wounds and limitations and that what you previously considered wounds or causes for resentment are actually blessings. (Does your beauty isolate you even while it attracts?)

The Sins of the Fathers

When I was seven, my parents wrote a letter to the archbishop of Virginia complaining that one of his schools would not accept their good Catholic daughter. The archbishop finally arranged for my admission, but that was no blessing for me. The kids whispered "nigger" and the teachers gave me low grades, assuming, I guess, that black skin comes thick. I wasn't brought up to hate whites and didn't understand all this. My father was a non-commissioned Army officer. He and my mother wanted money, nice cars, 2.5 college-educated kids, and a home of their own just like everyone else.

I clung to the idea that someone was going to help me get what I needed until the day I got my ass up to college and found myself tromping through the snow with borrowed books and no coat, freezing to death. I had to rethink things. I was in college to please my parents, but they weren't paying anything; I was tied to a series of scholarships; I was bored and uneasy. Suddenly I had no idea why I was doing any of it.

When I read W. E. B. Du Bois and Malcolm X and Eldridge Cleaver for the first time I started changing. I no longer wanted to accumulate things the way my parents did—just to show the neighbors they could do it. I joined the Black Student Union and for a while my hope was in pure Black Power, but when I found out that the Union was funded and controlled by whites and that our president kept a white girl on the side, I faded out. I stopped thinking *help your brothers* and started thinking *help yourself*. Racism was already institutionalized, Molotov cocktails or Civil Rights Amendments wouldn't change anything. I dropped out of school and got a secretarial job in another town.

I'm only twenty, but being black in America has already taught me to be a good jungle animal. I'm clever and flexible; I know how to change colors to get through hard situations. Yesterday, I walked into a drugstore and a wrinkled old lady looked at my afro and she says, "Why do you wear your hair like that? I think it's *disgusting!*" I had a dozen ways to respond. I could have mouthed her back, or ignored her, or mocked her by Uncle Tom-ing, but this old bitch was so dilapidated that I felt sorry for her. I looked straight into her scabby old eyes for a few seconds and walked out.

Being black in a white land means you've got to care a lot about yourself in order to survive. You either learn to stay on your toes or you get trampled. Every day I have to fight the stereotypes they lay on me, otherwise someday when I'm discouraged and someone suggests that my skin makes me dirty or stupid or lazy I might start believing it. Stereotypes are deadly for anyone. Counteracting mine keeps me flexible.

I don't believe in revenge, but I'm not going to help Whitey clean up his messes either. The Mafia shot heroin into the black ghettos and whites watched addicts flying off rooftops and said, "Good. That makes one less nigger!" But now that white GIs are getting wired, the big men suddenly decide they've got a drug problem! As far as I'm concerned, it would do them all good to walk around stoned for a while. . . . The reason I don't go in for revenge is that I know we all get paid back anyhow. There's a passage in the Bible that says, "The sins of the fathers are visited on the children," and I believe it. Maybe you don't pay immediately like George Wallace did, but sooner or later the chickens come to roost. We've all got relatives, and they all made stupid mistakes.

Sometimes I wish I could be loose and cool and let it all hang out like other kids these days. I'm so damn rational and serious, but how can I afford not to be? I know that, whatever I want done for myself, I've got to do. Later on I'll have time to luxuriate and count the times people put me down but now I'm working toward a time when people who want to live and let live can get together, clean out those who don't, and get down to it. And that revolution won't be all black. Look at me, my grandmother was Indian and my mother's family immigrated from the Caribbean someplace, so I don't even know where my color comes from! The truth is that no amount of money or tears can make up for the past, so why not let it go? Me, I'm getting ready for the good times!

HEROES AND VILLAINS

There are always good guys and bad guys. Stories and personalities would be dull without them. In myths the good guys are very good and the bad ones are dark (and interesting) as sin. It helps to exaggerate good and evil and to create clear targets because in real life the best and the worst are so entwined that we usually can't tell which is which. Dr. Jekyll and Mr. Hyde are in fact united. Exaggeration pulls apart what life joins together; because life is complex we invent heroes and heroines. We learn from churches, schools, and the media how to tell the white hats from the black hats; they instruct us as assiduously as any primitive mythology ever taught its adherents to locate the friends and enemies of God.

VIEWPOINTS

Trace the history of the heroes and heroines you have admired and imitated as personality models. Begin with your
earliest heroes and bring the tale up to the present. Whom
did you admire when you were five, fifteen, twenty-one?
Distinguish between official and unofficial heroes (your parents
may have been pleading the cause of St. Francis while you
were secretly riding with Robin Hood).

* What heroes and heroines did you find in books? In the
movies? In real life?
* What costumes did you wear?
* Whose speech did you imitate?
* If your heroes and heroines could speak to you now,
what advice would they give?
* What figures were held up to you as horrible villains?
* Who shares your current style of dress, speech, groom-
ing?
* Have your heroes and villains switched places over the
years? Why?

Heroes Don't Wear Glasses

My earliest heroes were all military figures in the traditional
Nordic mold. A hero was any person who received a mortal
wound and was subsequently borne away to Valhalla in the
arms of a statuesque blonde goddess or a government public
relations secretary. I memorized stories about Congressional
Medal of Honor winners, and for years was the star of
show-and-tell sessions. I nearly got to skip a grade when I
defined "posthumous" for my second-grade teacher.

When I realized that heroism was a dying business I looked around for a living hero. For a couple of years I was thoroughly enchanted by the exploits of John Glenn, who later became an astronaut. I realize that millions of kids thought of Glenn as a hero, but I knew who he was in the late fifties when he appeared on *Name That Tune* with Eddie Hodges, who later made a movie with Frank Sinatra about rubber trees. Glenn had just broken the transcontinental airspeed record in a Crusader Jet.

So by the time I entered second grade I had my whole life planned. I was going to be a test pilot and, if a war came along, an ace. My fame was secure. Then one day my mother took me to an optometrist. I sat in a dark room for a couple of hours and came home with a prescription for glasses, and it was not unlike a death in the family. Everyone knew the rules—you couldn't fly with glasses.

I can't say that I endured this mortal wound with any kind of nobility or grace. The day I got my glasses I sat in the parking lot searching for villains. I was past the age where I could blame the optometrist; I had betrayed myself. I sat there staring at a tree, seeing the individual leaves for the first time in my life. I thought about a heroic bomber pilot who, when he was shot down over the Pacific, ordered his crew to bail out and then flew his plane into the side of a Japanese battleship. I sat there looking at the tree, frustrated because I couldn't dive into what I saw. Clarity was my enemy.

I think this experience defined villainy for me. A villain was any person or event that prevented my dreams and wishes from coming true.

My next set of heroes came from television. Walt Disney had two western series featuring Texas John Slaughter and

El Fego Baca. Texas John wore white and married an innocent schoolmarm. He was good but not all that bright, depending on luck and the bias of his script writers to defeat evil. Baca was a shadowy, Zorro-type figure with nine lives. He was competent and willing to risk his life every other week. (In fact, half the fascination was seeing how he would live up to his own legend!) Of the two, Baca had the most effect on me, although I have to admit that part of me would like to flash around in white as an impersonal agent of good. I guess I ended up incorporating both—light and dark, honesty and cunning.

My last hero came from literature, the wizard Gandalf in Tolkien's *Lord of the Rings*. He gave me the idea that the hero goes through stages and that most magic takes place within the self. Gandalf is an intermediary between the world and the watchers. As Gandalf the Grey he fights his demon, dies, and is returned as Gandalf the White. By dying he makes connection with the watchers. That happens to me sometimes. Something dies and I confront the part of me that watches, the detached observer, the little boy looking at leaves. When I emerge I am better.

My personified villains are harder for me to remember. The television variety always disappeared after one show, dead or run out of town. I do remember once volunteering to go to hell and assassinate the Devil. When the minister turned down my proposal I realized that Sunday school wasn't telling the real story. A Christian credibility gap. If there wasn't a villain, then the battle between good and evil wasn't all it was cracked up to be.

In junior high school I had regular fights with most of the juvenile delinquents in town, but I didn't take these personally —we were representatives of two permanently opposed forces.

I was small, they were large: I was an egghead, they were tough, and we played our roles accordingly.

Gradually I'm learning that my worst enemies and best heroes are all within me. Whenever I try to shove that responsibility off on someone else, I get cut off from new possibilities. I'm like a citizen under old Chinese law who knows that if he kills a man he is responsible for the welfare of that man's family ever after. The burden of good and evil is mine. Knowing that, I do less worshiping these days. And if I met the Devil I'd probably apologize for listening to his detractors!

THE BELOVED ENEMY

Nietzsche said that you could measure the stature of a man by looking at his enemies. We are defined as much by our enemies as by our friends, as much by our negatives as by our positives. Just as the opposition between characters in a novel creates the drama, so a person's enemies give shape to the story of his life.

Enemies are dangerous because they consume energy and attention. Also, it's possible to become hypnotized by the thing we hate and stare at it for a lifetime. The energies of many societies and individuals are exhausted by hot and cold warfare. When being *against* becomes more important than being *with* or *for,* the enemy has destroyed the independence of your personality The person who defines his existence as a battle against Communists, blacks, whites, the Establishment, Jews, women, or Arabs forms a negative identity that indentures him to his enemy. A bad enemy destroys freedom, a good enemy provides the "loving combat" (Karl Jaspers) through which we can test and refine our values.

VIEWPOINTS

One way we perpetuate conflict is by making our wars holy wars, our enemies the enemies of God. A nation declares *"Gott mit uns,"* "In God we trust," and pronounces its enemies atheistic barbarians who threaten the foundations of civilization. We often conduct personal battles from a similar stance of self-righteousness. But when we see our enemies as fallible human beings driven by self-interest (like ourselves), warfare becomes more humane—a matter of conflicting interests.

If you look at your life as a drama, what conflicts shape the action?

* What Big Enemies have you fought in defense of God, humanity, country, race, or creed? What happened when the battle was won? Or lost?
* What ideas, causes, or institutions have you championed? What was in it for you? Would you do it again?
* Who is the enemy on your horizon?
* Describe scenes in your life when you were consumed by anger or frozen in hatred. What did you do? Did it achieve the kind of result you would have liked?

The Vestal Virgin Warrior

I grew up on a Kentucky farm deep in the heart of the Bible belt, and Scripture flowed out of me like boogy beat. My body was a wreck due to infantile paralysis, pneumonia, and assorted other ailments until my high school years when I began to train it into decent shape. When World War II broke out I wasn't planning to be a preacher any more but

I still believed "Thou shalt not kill." My father was ill and I
had an automatic draft deferment to work his farm, but
instead I went to Tennessee to write for a newspaper, determined to reflect the human face of America back to itself.
But in 1941 I saw *Sergeant York* in a local movie house and
everything turned around for me. York was a mountainman
who shot a Sharps rifle and singlehandedly captured a company of German soldiers in World War I, all the while quot-
ing the Epistle to the Romans on the necessity of combating
the agents of the Devil. Because of Sergeant York's Christian
dedication and my young reporter's quest to know (if I wasn't
blessed with the answers, then I would spend my life asking
the questions), I joined the Army at seventeen.

From then on I didn't get much sleep; I was pursuing
Hitler's forces with the fiercest concentration. I was made a
corporal in the artillery before I reached basic training, and
was assigned to intelligence and reconnaissance, which as-
sured my position on the front lines. Once an officer watched
me drill and suggested that I train at West Point but I de-
clined, afraid of missing the holy war. In the spring of 1945
when we liberated a German concentration camp at Ohrdruf
we found fresh stacks of machine-gunned Jews and Belgians.
This was the terrible, conclusive proof that my crusade was
on target. When the burgermeister from the next village was
brought to Ohrdruf to look at what he had probably guessed
but ignored, he hanged himself.

I trained myself like a precision lab instrument, effectively
eliminating large quantities of the enemy by taking carefully
calculated risks. I treated prisoners with a savagely cold
courtesy and went to great lengths to harden myself to the
dying. Once I ate my K rations while sitting on the ass of a
dead German. Another time, scouting in a wood with only a
pistol, I came upon a GI sitting upright with his head blown

off. He was still holding his rifle. I took it from his hands and thanked him out loud. He and I were intimate allies.

As soldier and forward observer I took a lot of personal risks and became something of a legend among the troops. They nicknamed me "Blood and Guts" after General Patton. The fact is, I loved combat with a kind of stupid innocence. I stayed on the lowest possible echelon of each maneuver in order to be in the front lines where there were no grays, no marginal considerations like food or status to worry about. The Army bureaucracy was so inept that it hardly ever reached the front lines, so we were free to fight our war the way we saw fit. My reputation for heroics paved my way; people expected king-sized deeds from me, and I delivered. The one or two times I shied away from taking the full, calculated risk I was miserable and ashamed. Nights I drank a lot, but always cemented myself together in the morning with calisthenics and oatmeal. Against the German enemy I could be totally committed, acting at the peak of my powers.

For me this was not a war of revenge. I was struggling to destroy an impersonal evil, not to inflict punishment. I stuck with God and prayed my way through scores of tight situations, repeating "Not my will but Thine be done" over and over. If I repeated this prayer enough times I was able to relax and enjoy the battle. I was a vestal virgin warrior, an honest soldier dedicated to defeating God's enemy.

The officers in our Army who lived rigidly by the rulebook were usually the same ones who cracked under fire or wasted precious energies collecting battle souvenirs. I held such men in great contempt, and still do. Pomposity in journalism or science or government—living by form instead of purpose—is the dominant characteristic of my enemies. In my present work I spend a lot of time encouraging folks to play over their heads, to stop collecting souvenirs and rise to their own

dreams. It's like the time I commanded a ground-survey
team in a war zone and acted as the hot-coffee waiter. Since
I didn't know any trigonometry myself, I toted a submachine
gun with my wares so the men could work safely through
the cold nights, and they did exceptional work. As their
servant I was terribly proud of them. Ever since the war,
people who rise full-hearted to the task of living have been my
fighting allies.

PUNCTUATING TIME: Rites of Passage

Timerunsonandonwithneverapauseorvariation   but   human
time is broken into manageable units. We create minutes,
days, weeks, months, and years to punctuate the unbroken
flow. We mark the beginning, middle, and end of things to
find ourselves in time. Personal time is limited by the inevitability of death, so we invent clocks and anniversaries and
holidays and decades to create the illusion of stasis in a fluid
universe. We divide time to conquer it.

Our inner time sense records intensity and importance
rather than duration: an October afternoon of love among
the dunes may be written larger in memory than all the weeks
surrounding it. When you put together the story of your life
you face the central question of how to punctuate time. What
moments will you isolate and give symbolic importance,
single out for dramatic effect? To make a coherent story from
the undifferentiated mass of your experience you need to
divide the flow of time with a comma, a period, a paragraph,
a section, a chapter.

Every person's autobiography is both unique and usual, the
story of an individual life and of all mankind. We are shaped
by an inescapable human condition which dictates certain

events and themes that will figure prominently in every life story.

Most cultures create rites of passage to celebrate an individual's transition from one stage of life to the next. Baptism or circumcision may mark the passage from womb to membership in the tribe. Initiation ordeals or menstruation signal the end of adolescence and entrance into the adult world. Marriage and procreation may signify acceptance of mature responsibilities. And death is the doorway to heaven, oblivion, or rebirth.

The practice of ritualizing the standard divisions between the stages of life reflects an ancient wisdom about the care and management of crisis and trauma. Transitions are turbulent times. Sudden changes in body chemistry and social expectations—for instance at the onset of adolescence or toward the end of life—may cause radical changes in personality. The way an individual negotiates major identity crises depends to a large extent on how these crises are defined and valued by his society. If crisis is taken as a sign of sickness or disintegration the transitions will be accompanied by anxiety, loneliness, and shame. If they are seen as signs of growth they may be experienced with excitement and pride. For instance, primitive ordeals of initiation (fasting, endurance tests, the killing of an enemy or wild animal) focus adolescent anxiety on a task which can be performed with pride.

Perhaps the clearest indication of the dignity pre-modern societies afforded the transition crises is in the widespread tales of the journey of the hero. The hero—the dragon killer, shaman, Siddhartha, Christ, Orpheus—must face a radical loss and rediscovery of identity. The story is told in many idioms but always the hero forsakes comfort, security, and certainty when he plunges into the dark habitation of the powers of evil. While in the underworld he fights with a

demon or devil, and is often crucified. But eventually he
rises from the dead and returns to the ordinary world with
enlightenment and power. In the hero legends the promise
is clear: any person who dares the radical descent into the
chaos that lies beneath the veneer of personality and civilization has a chance of returning with a whole soul.

In modern society the rites for marking the divisions between the stages of life are mechanical, ill defined, or non-
existent. We don't punctuate clearly enough. Going to school
is sometimes regarded as initiation into the community beyond the home. Sex or a job or a driver's license are the
tokens of graduation into the initial stages of adult life. Credit
cards and a mortgage are signs of the full responsibility of
maturity. Between maturity and retirement we do not expect
to have identity crises. Those persons who do have "nervous
breakdowns," neuroses, or emotional illnesses are sent to
psychiatrists or tranquilized; they are made to feel ashamed
of their trauma. Our definition of the hero's journey as
neurosis or psychosis adds guilt, loneliness, and despair to
transitions which could be creative events.

VIEWPOINTS

Discovering your identity, organizing your life story, punctuating your time involves dividing your life into stages.

* Choose ten scenes from your past which were important
pivotal events in your life and describe them. Detail the
circumstances, characters, and backgrounds of each scene.
How are the scenes you have chosen representative of your
present life? How did they change or affect you? How has
your view of them altered over the years?
* Make an outline of your autobiography. What are the

major divisions? Chapter titles? Subsections? The title of
the book? What stages does your life naturally seem to fall
into? What ages were "crisis" periods for you?

* When did you cease to be a child? When did you cease to
be young? When did you become mature? When did you
become old?

* What personal, family, and social rituals or celebrations
were involved in changing stages?

* After you've done an initial outline of your autobiography put it aside and do another that uses entirely different
organizing principles, chapter titles, pivotal events, key persons, and time scales. Turn your story inside out; try a new
way of punctuating your time. If your life story has the feel
of a tragedy flip it over and make it a comedy; if it sounds
like a romance change the tone slightly so that it is ironic;
if it has a pathetic ring turn it into a hero tale.

* How do you envision punctuating your time in the future?

I'm Glad I Don't like Spinach

From the very beginning I was attracted to boys instead
of girls, but I felt terribly guilty about it. I thought my feelings were dreadful, sinful, perverted; I was the only boy in the
world who wanted the things I did. I was bad, bad, bad and
would surely go to hell.

But when I was fourteen I broke through all that by making
love with Howie—an older kid who lived down the street—
and that one experience showed me what was natural to me.
You read all kinds of stuff saying that a homosexual experience is a horrible thing for a young boy, it cripples him
for life and so on. In my case, that wasn't the result. It was a
pretty cataclysmic experience, but what I got out of it was a
tremendous feeling of relief, you know, I found out I wasn't

alone, that there were other people who liked what I did and therefore I couldn't be such a big sinner! After that "rite of passage" I felt tremendously at ease with my sexual feelings. I knew what I wanted, and I knew with whom too!

During that time Mother hung a light which was really an old tin lantern punched full of holes on the front porch. It didn't give much light and wasn't worth a damn, but Mother was quite pleased with it. I remember the day she showed it to my older brother. He looked at it and said, "It doesn't give much light, but it's probably good enough for Leo and Howie to sit out under at night!" I didn't know how much any of them knew during those years, but as long as I could go on doing as I pleased it didn't really matter.

I can't imagine what my life would have been like if I hadn't been gay. I just never think of it, it doesn't enter my head, though I'm sure I wouldn't like it! It's like that joke about the kid who said, "I'm glad I don't like spinach because if I did I'd *eat* the awful stuff!" I'm happy with my appetites the way they are, pretty much like I found them at fourteen.

Folks I Have Known and How They Moved Me

INTRODUCTION:

I lost my father and my mother wasn't available much. So I grew like a weed in whatever soil I found around me.

Chapter One Grandma Murphy

Grandma supervised my piano lessons, starched and ironed my dresses, and sent me to school with a powdered nose and Evening in Paris dabbed behind each ear. She was herself a perfect lady except for one quirk: Grandma had this huge mound of dried dog shit that she treasured like a rare gem. Usually she used it as a doorstop, but when the nuns came calling she always placed it smack in the center of the living-room rug.

Moral: Even perfect ladies have their idiosyncrasies.

Chapter Two Sister Prudentia

When a boy in my kindergarten class wet his pants and burst into tears Sister Prudentia called his parents. His mother and father came at once, kissed him, shook hands with the sister, and took the kid home with them. I thought it a wonderful scene and wet my chair the same afternoon. Even though I cried real tears Sister Prudentia would have none of it. She made me stay on the flooded chair the rest of the day. And after that I had to walk home from school with my skirt hanging wet in front of everyone.

Moral: What works for your brother may not work for you.

Chapter Three Mrs. Garbey

For a while my sister and brother and I lived in a boardinghouse. The managers used food for bribes and punishment, so I always felt a little bit hungry. One day my third-grade teacher, Mrs. Garbey, asked me to carry her lunch bag out to the garbage can. I did, and she asked me to do it every day after that. I would go directly into the girls' room and gobble up the fresh milk and sandwiches that were always in the brown bag. Mrs. Garbey never said a word about these extended missions, but soon there were cookies in the bag too.

Moral: (There isn't one. It's just that true gifts are always remembered.)

Chapter Four Gail Henley

The Henley family lived way outside of town and didn't believe in bathing for some reason, so Gail was the butt of many eighth-grade jokes. I set out to befriend her and gradually induced her to wash after gym class with soapy paper towels. But when Gail responded by inviting me to spend a week end with her strange family I made up an excuse and backed off. I was scared of getting contaminated, and after that I felt too guilty to speak of her.

Moral: If you convert someone to the one true path, don't be shocked when she starts to identify with you.

Chapter Five Joe DiMaggio

More than anything I wanted to be a boy and a professional baseball player. But the closest I ever came to it was the day Joe DiMaggio came to town and I touched his right buttock in a crowd. It was wonderful, but not magical. Finally I had to give up my dreams and resign myself to being a girl.

Moral: Society has plans for you long before you arrive.

Chapter Six Sid Breslin

His friends said he was infatuated with me, but I just couldn't believe it. True, I was a pretty ornament on his arm, but I hadn't heard of half the titles on his bookshelves and felt abysmally average around him and his bright friends. I worried and hesitated too long, and finally he threw up his hands and I fell out. That's when I decided that it must have been love.

Moral: If you pay enough attention to your inferiority feelings they'll probably come true.

Chapter Seven Duke Cleveland

A quick look at his life story would tell you that the man had suffered. And a look at the long string of deluded women in his life would tell you that they'd suffered too. But I believed in his struggles and his causes, and in my ability to be different from the other women. I was wrong: I lost heart,

weight, humor, and nearly my life before I got up and walked
away. It might have helped if we'd liked each other.
*Moral: If you persist in confusing a person with a cause,
they'll both run away with you.*

Epilogue:

My life has been full of sad, dramatic experiences. But I
dread the pathos of it all, so I tend to break them down into
quick, wry episodes. The chapters in my autobiography flash
like sixty-second sparklers in a black night! I'm probably
afraid that if I let them drag on they will drag me down and
turn other people off; humor is so much more appealing
than heaviness. And yet, looking back with a laugh means
that whole hunks of reality get edited out. My mother, for instance, hardly appears here, because she's pathetic enough to
turn the whole thing into a tragedy. Still, the story is to be
continued, and next time I do this I think I'll let more in and
skip the moral conclusions: maybe by now the sorrow in my
life can mix with the comedy without poisoning everything.

V

THE FUTURE
You Are What You Want

Time shapes our present the way a sculptor shapes unworked clay, molding each moment between the right hand of the past and the left hand of the future. What we remember characterizes us as uniquely as our thumbprints. What has happened to us molds us as certainly as what has not. An amalgam of the known and the unknown, of fact and possibility, makes up what we call ourselves.

A generation ago planning for the future was *the* mark of maturity. Now it's a little suspect: since no one knows what the future will be, thinking about it aborts awareness of what is happening now. Why not live today and let tomorrow take care of itself? But, while children can live in an eternal now where desire and satisfaction are near neighbors, most of us have too many unsatisfied desires to be content with the moment. We want more than we now have. We demand of the future some imagined fullness that presently eludes us. We want to grow, to experience more, to be more. There is always something we want and don't have: a lover, a Mercedes-Benz, a shack in the country, high cheekbones. We chase absent satisfactions; surely, someday we will be nearer to perfection, to the furtive desires we have stored in tomorrow. Or will we?

What do we want? What fulfillment could satiate the desire that motivates human striving? Augustine thought the restless heart could find its peace only in God. Marx was certain it would find a homeland in the proletarian state. Freud suggested that our true desires are repressed and unconscious and we really want to return to the security of the womb. In our discontent we try to quiet desire with religion, romance, status, sensation, food, or fame, but we are never filled. The wanting remains.

The question is perennial: can desire be satisfied? Eastern philosophers and religious thinkers tend to believe that it cannot; Nirvana is found when desire is extinguished. Western psychologists are generally more pragmatic and optimistic. They work on the assumption that, if individuals can unmask their desires and discover what they are, they may achieve happiness.

If we unearth our unconscious desires and lay them alongside our conscious ones we can trace the anatomy of our desires and learn something about the source of our conflicts. Some desires can be fulfilled while others endure in the form of fantasies. Stories and myths help to excite and clarify them. Any mythical portrait which a culture projects (Buddha, Socrates, Jesus, Jane Fonda, Mick Jagger, Jackie Kennedy Onassis) promises its imitators a satisfying style of life.

Fantasies, dreams, daydreams, and future plans are also excellent divining rods for locating underground desires. Our wildest and tenderest desires hide out in our imaginations, emerging when sleep, drugs, or strong feeling loosen the rational censorship we call common sense. Long-repressed desires turn everything topsy-turvy when they emerge. As Chuang-tze said: "Last night I dreamt I was a butterfly. Now I don't know whether I am a butterfly dreaming I am a man, or a man dreaming I am a butterfly." But when the voices of darkness are welcomed into the light a new harmony sounds between the unconscious and the conscious. And then satisfaction may be just a moment away.

DEATH: The Awful Certainty

The only event we can predict with virtual certainty is the one we least like to think about—our own death. Death is the doorway to the future, the one fact in a world otherwise governed by probabilities. Before we can fantasize freely about our futures we have to break the death barrier; confront the ambivalent feelings that cluster around our images of the end.

Modern people don't die; they just pass away. Soldiers take care of our killing and undertakers do our burying, preferably discreetly. Classical philosophers insisted that wisdom and happiness were only possible after a person had come to terms with the inevitability of death. Plato defined philosophy as training for dying. If we evade death we avoid the event that sets the definitive limits on our mortality; we cling to the illusion that there's an eternity of time in which to do the things we lack courage to do today. Death disillusions by reminding us that we arise from and return to the earth (humus). It makes us human by confronting us with the fragility of life and the need for decision.

For the human animal there is no purely biological act. Death (like birth or sex) is surrounded with interpretations

and explanations. We need to understand what death means
and why people should die. Throughout the course of history
the myths, images, and metaphors used to interpret death reflect a profound ambiguity. It is never clear whether death is
friend or enemy, the beginning or the end of life.

Either death is: an end to life; the ultimate enemy; the
grim reaper; the castrator. In the Christian tradition, as in
many ancient myths, death enters the world as a punishment
for transgression against some divine law. Man dies because
he ate the forbidden fruit or because he broke a taboo or
stole fire from the gods. If there were no enmity between
man and the gods, no alienation, there would be no death.

Or death is: a prelude to rebirth; the hidden friend; the
womb of life; the lover. In cultures where the feeling for nature remains strong human life is seen as analogous to the life
of plants and death is viewed as one stage in an eternal cosmic
cycle. In the winter of his life man dies in order that he may
be reborn in the spring. The Hopi Indians symbolize this by
burying their dead in the fetal position. In the end we come
back to the beginning.

Different psychological realities underlie these two estimates
of death. We experience death only as observers. A dying person experiences dying but, presumably, not death. The survivors observe a lifeless body and experience grief, relief,
anger, and panic. To an observer death seems final. It steals
away a unique person whose life can never be restored or repeated. If we have loved the dead person death seems the
final enemy of love and life. When we think about our own
death we are inundated by the images and fears that sur-
round an imaginary future event. But we confront our feelings about death most directly when we come face to face
with any radical change in our lives. Something in us (the
ego, the infantile self, the first-born self) does not believe we

can survive fundamental changes in personality structure or life circumstances, and so each crisis in life is shadowed by death. Then when we survive the crisis we realize that change may mean metamorphosis rather than death. The ego dies and a stronger self is born. Then it may come to us that death is only a gateway to wider life, the final trip beyond the prison of the ego.

Speculations and explanations always pale before the reality of death. In the end we have to face it raw. We can escape obsession with death by paying attention to the appeals of living. It is unlived life that makes fear of death persistent and morbid. We might even see our death as a gift to the living: nature decrees that the father dies so the child can inherit his full place in the sun. Even the death of those we love is not a total loss. Death adds the bass notes to the symphony. By our grief for what is missing we know the terrible value of what was once present among us.

Maybe the best we can do is struggle against death as if it were our final enemy, refuse to "go gentle into that good night," affirm the priority of light over darkness. Then, in that penultimate moment (when, it is said, our life flashes before us and we know that it was good), we may allow death to turn its other face toward us and know that it is a friend. Maybe.

VIEWPOINTS

If you want to feel what death means to you, take a look at your favorite death fantasies.

* How do you most frequently see yourself dying?
* Who died the way you expect to die?

* What habits may dictate your style of dying? (Smoking, drinking, commuting, worrying, sky diving?)
* When will you die? Who died at this age?
* Why are you going to die? Is death a failure? A depletion of energy? A natural conclusion to life? Do you die to make more room for the living? Because your body is worn out? Because you are bored, frustrated, despairing? Because you are satisfied?
* What is your dominant attitude toward death—defiance, acceptance, fear, longing, sorrow, curiosity?

Imagine you died yesterday and look back on your life. You died with many dreams unfulfilled.

* What accomplishments, relationships, moments mean most?
* What are your regrets? What have you left undone that you wanted to do? What have you done that you wish you hadn't?

Death wears many faces. When the young die death is tragedy; when the old or incurably ill die it is deliverance; when our enemies die it is retribution and justice.

* What moods and emotions have dominated your experience of the death of others? (Grief, anger, fear, relief?)
* Whose death would cause you the greatest sorrow? Whose would give you the greatest pleasure? Who would care the most if you died?

In the world of myth death is usually considered an unnatural event, a strangeness in need of an explanation. Here is an African myth that tells why death came into the world.

Formerly men had no fire but ate all their food raw. At that time they did not need to die for when they became old God made them young again. One day they decided to beg God for fire. They sent a messenger to God to convey their request. God

replied to the messenger that he would give him fire if he was
prepared to die. The man took the fire from God, but ever since
then all men must die. (Darasa, Gada.)[1]

    * Make up your own myth about why we must die.

The Death Machine

    It used to be that every time I drove on a freeway death
was right behind me. It was a silver Mercedes cutting into
my lane; or a Mack truck barreling up from behind, squish-
ing me like a blister; or sometimes an overpass would give
way, burying me in great heaps of concrete. I was always at
the wheel when these things happened, driving too fast,
straining to outrun the Death Machine. . . . Later death
stopped haunting the freeway and moved into the world of
disease. Now I was losing great quantities of weight, or my
blood was drying up, or my muscles caved in on April 1.
Everyone else was terribly shocked, but once I felt death
pumping through my veins, I let go easily. I saw myself turn
to the wall, dying with my eyes open.

    Which brings me to suicide, my secret death. That fantasy
comes in two versions. One suicide is a crazed plea for attention, a calculated demand that the world pay for my
frustrations. In this fantasy I can't quite die: death spits me
back, leaving me with ugly scars, stunned friends, and another perspective. The other suicide is a clean, active ending,
a match I carry in my pocket in case of a blizzard, my way
of assuming (or presuming) as much power over my death
as I have in my life. I detect the fingers of that fantasy in a lot
of literature. Camus finally drove into a tree, Virginia Woolf
walked into water, Mayakovsky blew his head off, Sylvia

[1] Susan Feldmann, ed., *African Myths and Tales* (Dell Publishing Co.,
New York, 1963), p. 121.

Plath opened the gas oven and left a note for the maid. Suicide seduces me with its drama and relief, but at the same time it's terribly sad, a robber. I wish those artists were still around heating up the world.

And then I think of Picasso, running up and down stairs and making perfect paintings until he was ninety-one, and I know there are active ways of living as well as dying. The fact is, most of the time when I want to die it's because I'm not as *alive* as I want to be and death would at least blot the disappointment. My freeway deaths have to do with feeling desperately competitive and overpowered (high gear ain't good enough); death by disease is final proof that we're nothing but victims in a deadly world. That ending lets me off the hook. It says, "See? Why fight and love and work when it all can be canceled in an instant!"

But when I step back and look at my bones and my luck and my string of octogenarian relatives munching pork chops I see that I'm probably destined (doomed, maybe) to live a long life. It's not as if I'm royalty threatened by court intrigues, or some rare, frail beauty too sensitive to stay alive. At eighty (knock on wood!) I'll probably be rocking on a porch somewhere, watching the young folks slugging it out, creaking toward senility, my old crone death rocking away beside me.

If You're on Your Way to the Morgue

Death can belt you pretty hard, but if you're done loving somebody, it's nothing but a trip to the morgue.

The day I went to the D.C. morgue to identify my husband's body I couldn't even find the place. I was looking for a cool gray tomb like all the rest of those official buildings but none of them matched the number they'd told me over the phone. Finally I flagged a cab and the driver (a real nice-looking man with smooth dark skin) nearly dropped his teeth. "Why lady," he said, "the morgue's just around the corner!" We were both laughing about mislocating the morgue just because it was bright red brick like a Methodist church, and then the cabby says, "If you're on your way to the morgue, how come you're so happy?"

Well, I was laughing because I once did love my man, I knew when I had it and I knew when it was gone. Before we were married he was gentle and respectful as any man I've ever met. I wouldn't sleep with him before we were married but he didn't leave me. He just went on working hard and taking me to movies until I got good and ready to hitch up. But after that everything changed. He started putting down a lot of beer, and then other stuff, stepping out with women and hollering at me when I asked him about it. One day while I was ironing he stormed in, grabbed the iron, and laid it steaming hot on my upper arm. Well, I couldn't love that man any more. I couldn't even recognize him. I kicked him out of the house and that was that.

I gave the driver a dollar, gathered up my nerve, and went into the morgue. A fat man with a beltful of keys (I guess he was caretaker of all those drawers of dead bodies) led me to room 127. He stood there rolling out my husband's chilled corpse, looking bored as anything. I was standing maybe ten feet away and couldn't get a good look at the dead man's face but I said, "Yeah, that's him," turned on my heel, and got the hell out of there.

I'll tell you this: I sure hope it *was* John Carter Lockwood lying there dead. If not, some poor lady's gonna be worrying her head for nothing, and I'm likely to end up living that bad dream all over again!

Who's Worrying?

From the scientific point of view, death is a question without an answer, and therefore it is not a valid concern. In the
broader sense, there really isn't any death. Atoms persist. Just
as the car I'm driving has some molecules of steel that were
probably once running around in a 1936 Ford, some of the
carbon atoms in my body will exist in some other body later
on. But that mechanism won't be me. You see, what is me?
Me is only my present consciousness. I exist only as a series of
metabolic connections in the brain that call up certain experiences in retrospect, perceiving an order that will someday
disappear.

For some reason which we don't understand there has to
be a beginning and an end to things. If all the mutants that
ever lived were still alive you would have one hell of a situation! Death is simply a natural part of the life cycle. One
hundred fifty years from now absolutely everyone who lives
today will be gone, all three billion of us, and what will matter?

Death is only important to youth, who are attracted to the
things they haven't done yet, or to people who are frustrated
in their work and don't want to cash in until they at least get
some pleasure out of life. But people who are involved in what
really gives them pleasure just don't have that fear. When
I'm solving theorems I'm not worrying about anything. What's
important is the minimization of pain and the optimization of
local pleasure.

Death is an abstract thing, almost as abstract as life itself.
I'll probably never have to experience my own death. I am
not the same person I was five years ago. I'm in a constant
state of metamorphosis, so that my life is not a precipitous

thing. And when I reach old age (if I do) one of two things will happen: I will go quickly or I will have evolved into senility or senescence, in which case I won't be me. For all I know, that old man will welcome death. I don't want it now but if I dropped dead tomorrow it wouldn't bother me. If it happens it happens. It's not something I think about. I'm concerned with the next moment, with what I can do tomorrow.

You mean other people really worry about death?

THE ART OF FANTASY

Imagination is an incorrigible child forever at play with frivolities when reason is doing serious work. Daydreams wander in and out of consciousness, interrupting concentrated thought. As rationality gains exclusive control over our lives we drive out our daydreams. They are flights from reality into fancy, trips taken at the expense of the boss, the job, the problem that has to be solved. All true. Daydreams deliver us into the private world of unfulfilled desire and let us taste forbidden pleasures that are sweeter than work, duty, responsibility, honor, gentility, and moderation. They are disturbers of the peace, but we ignore them at our own peril. Without them the psyche shrivels.

The more we know about the kaleidoscopic worlds of desire the more we are likely to be able to make satisfying choices. Desires range from split-second spasms to lifelong intentions. Some desires lead to action; others linger or wear themselves out in fantasy. Imagine a scale of desire. The weakest desires are fleeting wishes, such as: "I wish I could fly, change sexes for a week, eat chocolate every day . . ." Wants are one degree stronger than wishes: "I really want to have a baby, write a book, learn to ski." Willing and deciding are manifestations of even stronger desires: "I probably won't become President but I will write a book." Action is the final stage in the realization of desire: "I decided to write and am typing this paragraph." There is no reason to assume that all desires must end in action, but it helps to know which of our wishes to ripen into wants, which wants to deepen into decisions, and which decisions to actualize.

Fantasy can be an economical way of trying on alternative ways of feeling, acting, and being. In the safety of the imagination we can become Charles Manson and purge our murderous rage without shedding blood, or make love to anyone without the entanglement of an actual relationship, or play God without having to reckon with the Devil. In fantasy any outlawed or unacceptable wish can find fulfillment. We can be as cruel, crazy, strong, weak, grandiose, timid, or whimsical as we please.

Paradoxically, when we stay in touch with our most outrageous fantasies our path toward realistic goals is most direct. When we allow the child within us free play it is easier to enjoy our self-chosen responsibilities.

VIEWPOINTS

Your fantasy life can tell you much about your unfulfilled wishes. Discover where your mind wanders when it slips away from grim reality. The next time you're stuck in a meeting or a concert hall and can't concentrate, let your fantasies fly and watch where they go. (Are you killing the boss? Eating? Making love? Being applauded? Winning someone over to your side?) If you don't force your daydreams into rational or moral categories they will take you fantastic places.

Planned fantasy trips are another way of exploring the imagination. Try these archetypal scenes.

* While hiking in the mountains you notice a cave in a wall of granite. You crawl up to the opening and look into the darkness. In the distance you hear running water and a voice calling, "Let me out. Let me out." And . . .

* On an average morning in early May you receive a letter informing you that Howard Hughes has left you his entire estate. After recovering from the shock (and calculating the amount left after taxes) you decide that the first thing you'll do is . . .

* Create a sexual fantasy in which you are totally satisfied.

* Imagine that you can travel freely inside your body in the manner of Isaac Asimov's *Fantastic Voyage*. Walk throughout your entire body and describe what you see.

* You accidentally take a drug that erases all inhibitions and morality for one week, along with your accountability. You are perfectly free. What do you do for seven days?

* You are invisible for a few days. What do you do?

Design a utopian society that could conceivably exist in your future.

* How is society governed?
* What are the sexual, religious, and political mores?
* Who works? When? For what?
* How and by whom are children raised and educated?

Play God and make this the best of all possible worlds.

* What do you change, and what remains the same? (Are there time and space? Are there human beings? Minds? Bodies? Is there pain? Tension? Death?)
* What do creatures live for?

Life Could Be a Dream

Playing God is an old role for me; I already tried it once and failed. When I was seventeen I figured out there wasn't any God and decided to become a scientist. If there's no God and no absolute values, what is there except survival? So I made up my mind to work on the problem of aging. I knew that immortality was a farfetched idea but science was our one hope so I ran after it anyway. I zoomed through the biology doctoral program and went right to work for a prominent research foundation. By the time I was twenty-five I was considered an expert on the science of aging but it was beginning to look like a poor proposition; I began to suspect that aging was not a disease that was likely to be cured in my lifetime. And to complicate matters further, I discovered people. I fell in love and saw that beauty is mixed in with mystery and that the universe is much more complex than my logical positivist training allowed for. Reality can't be caught in a net of Euclidian logic and verifiable hypotheses. At the ripe old age of twenty-seven I left the aging business and began to explore mortality.

Now I'm not sure I like the idea of being God, it's too much responsibility and gravity. But if I *was* God I'd make some changes. First I'd wipe out cruelty. I'd be like a benign General Motors recalling defective models, eliminating all those people who spend their lives making war or making other people miserable. Basic structures like time, space, sex, bodies, and Chicago could remain much as they are; the main thing I'd do is take the load off people by teaching them to separate their bodies from their souls. Right now I know we are spirits, but I'm not sure we could exist without bodies.

If we could, everything would be possible. We could park our bodies, take an astral flight, and come back for them later. We could take little trips inside other people's minds and see how they worked without losing our own identities. And unless we bogged down in pride or stubbornness, we'd never have to get stuck in outer space, in the grave, in Anaheim, California, or even in love.

If people could only be taught to separate body and soul, life would be like a dream. The dream world is a great place because if you know you're dreaming you can go ahead and enjoy the action without being responsible for the consequences. You just wake up and poof! it's all gone. The other night I (not God now but me, the mortal) had a fantastic dream like that. I'm riding my bicycle down the Seventh Street hill and can't control the damn thing. It won't brake, won't quite steer, and it looks like I'm going to crash over the cliff at the end. I'm panicked trying everything I can think of to get control until suddenly I realize I'm in a dream. Then I think: if I'm in a dream I can't get killed, and it's not every day that I get a chance to ride my bike over a cliff! So I let go of the brakes and relax. I expect to drop down the cliff and break some bones maybe, but when I hit the first landing the bike bounces up and soars off over the ocean! If I was God I'd teach people to sit back and enjoy their flights!

But I'm not so sure about death any more: maybe life wouldn't be so rich if we didn't think this was our only trip. I guess what I'd do if I was God is let people avoid their deaths (indefinitely, but not forever) by being able to leave their bodies at will. Meanwhile, human minds would inevitably be devising more and more fantastic tricks for themselves, which would keep us all entertained. Life on earth would be rich as a dream—and *almost* eternal!

DREAMS

In dreams we live a thousand lives. When sleep conquers reason we become omnipotent; like Proteus, we change form to experience the beasts and little children that roam within us.

Psychology has rediscovered what ancient and primitive peoples knew: that dreams are essential for sanity. Greek seers, Roman emperors, and Egyptian pharaohs used dreams to decipher the future. Many American Indians consulted dreams to learn when they should feast or take to the warpath. Job thought that dreams were songs God gave us in sleep. Freud saw them as the royal road to the unconscious. Recent experiments have shown that persons deprived for several nights of the part of sleep in which dreaming takes place become anxious and disassociated. A healthy human mind seems to operate on two levels, the realistic and the fantastic, the conscious and the unconscious. Like a live virus, the chaos of playful fantasy inoculates us against serious madness.

These days we pay sparse attention to the one third of our lives we live in sleep. The rationality that dominates our culture is concentrated on conquering the outer world, thrusting toward craters on the moon. When volcanoes erupt in our inner spaces we label them emotional disturbances, or psychotic episodes, and try to seal them off with tranquilizers or therapy. Modern culture is permeated by a deep, unspoken moralism that is evident in our suspicions of free love, free association, free schools, and free dreams.

Whenever the unconscious is opened up, whether by psychoanalysis, psychedelic drugs, or exaggerated attention to

dreams, there is danger of getting stuck in memories of ancient injuries or staying forever among the lotus-eaters feed-
ing on the nectar of fantasies. The inward journey is most
enriching for the traveler who brings the visions of the night
into the light of day.

VIEWPOINTS

Dreams are like people: they respond to attention and retreat
when neglected. Keep a notebook by your bed and write
down as many of your dreams as you can. If you wake in the
night assume the position you were in while dreaming and
sink back into semi-sleep. Keep the scenes you remember
from the dream on the edge of your awareness and the whole
thing may revive. With practice you can learn to recall
panoramic dreams in full living color. Save a few minutes
before going to sleep and before getting up to simmer in bed;
the timeless area between waking and sleeping is particularly
fertile for cultivating dreams.

Here are some dreaming clues:

* Dreams are mysteries which nobody knows how to interpret. Theories about why we dream and what dreams mean
are only theories. Dreams may be waste products of the
mind, voices of the dead, solutions to crossword puzzles, or
flashes from the future.

* Enjoy your dreams. At the very least they are playthings
of the mind. If you assign them a single meaning they are
likely to evade you.

* Share your dreams. They are free gifts, so why not pass
them on?

* Who appears in your dreams? Often? Why do you think
they are there?

* There is no complete interpretation of any part of a dream. If you dream that you're riding a horse down a woody path with serpents circling your body it may symbolize desire for sex, or freedom, or greater control over wild instincts. Or someone may be rocking the bed. All or none of these things may be true. Play with different possible meanings.

* Interpret one dream in the light of others. Look for symbols and themes that appear over a long period of time. A series of dreams about cops or caves will add force and clarity to your understanding of what these things symbolize for you.

* Cultivate an active relationship to your dreams. If a dream disturbs you or feels unfinished, decide to dream it again and see where it goes. Sometimes this works.

* Everything in a dream is a creation of your mind, a projection of some aspect of your personality (e.g., if your mother appears in a dream she may represent the maternal part of yourself). Fritz Perls, one of the creators of Gestalt therapy, suggests that we turn our dreams into psychodramas in which we play the role of every character or aspect. *I am an old house, I am barren, without ornament or beauty. I sit in the middle of a lonely field by myself. No one visits me any more. . . . Be* each element in your dream.

* Pay special attention to recurring scenes, childhood dreams, and the most frightening and pleasant dreams you can remember.

House of Horrors (A Dream)

I'm in the front room of a huge old layered house. There's a woman with dark skin and short dark hair standing by the window. She's wearing a plain black skirt and a white babydoll blouse that sticks out in front because she's pregnant.

I've never seen her before. I go up to her and start kicking and shoving, gently at first and then harder. She doesn't fight back and I keep it up, poking her from room to room. Finally she locks herself in the downstairs bathroom and suddenly there are three or four faceless people with me outside the door. I know she's trapped in there and, sure enough, we bust the lock with no trouble. The woman is standing in the corner by the tub. I say to the others, "Let's give it to her," and we start beating her savagely. I keep punching her belly with my fist, over and over, and she just stands there with her eyes closed, her arms flapping like rags in the wind. I open the medicine cabinet and take out five pairs of miniature scissors with sharp, tiny legs and hand them out to everyone. Between punches we poke them into her upper body. Every place we sink them two little red pools of blood appear on the soft white cotton in perfect circles, and I think it's pretty, I like watching them rise slowly to the surface. All this time the woman just pushes us back gently; she's taking it, just taking it. Eventually we whip her back into the front room. We're getting ready to leave, so I tell the lackeys to tie her into the chair with a piece of rope. Then she speaks and asks if I will please tie her lying on the sofa so that she can bear her child. Then for the first time I think about the consequences—the human consequences—of this thing. How will she get the kid out or cut the umbilical cord if her hands are tied? I tell the others, "Tie her on the sofa with her arms free, turn out the lights, lock all the doors, and yank out the phone." Then I take off, leaving everybody behind. I'm running down the street trying to get far away.

House of Horrors Revisited (A Psychodrama)

FRIEND: Assume that your dream is a drama between the different parts of yourself. Get inside the characters and let them talk to each other. First be the tormentor, the one you call "I."

TORMENTOR TO MOTHER: We're beating you and stabbing you all around your soft white heart and you pretend it isn't happening, you don't respond. Why don't you fight back? If you would respond maybe we would stop tormenting you.

(*Mother keeps silent.*)

TORMENTOR TO BABY: And you, so protected in there, all curled up riding on somebody else; it'll be different when you come out! But it's your mother I'm really after, not you. She's so self-righteous, so silent.

MOTHER TO TORMENTOR: I don't know why you're doing this. I don't even know you. But this will pass. . . . It's like childbirth, if I can hold myself together I know it will pass. . . . You can't destroy the life in me.

FRIEND: Say that again.

MOTHER: You can't destroy the life in me. You can't destroy the life in me! You can hurt me but you can't destroy the life that's in my body. The only way you can touch that is by killing me and you won't do that, you're too small, you don't care enough to kill me, so all I have to do is endure. I have something you don't have, that's why you're doing this. You think the pools of blood are pretty because you've never had anything beautiful inside yourself. I hardly feel what you're doing to me: I'm thinking about my child and when she starts coming there's nothing any of you can do, you're just bringing it on faster, you're bringing my child out, which is what I want.

FRIEND: Your voice is so weak and childlike that it cancels the force of what you're saying. Try being the baby in the womb; let yourself go all the way into feelings of passivity.

BABY: It's so nice and soft and thick and warm in here. There's some pressure from the outside but it doesn't hurt me, it feels like a liquid massage. Still, I think they're trying to get me to come out of here, and I don't want to.

FRIEND: Well, tell them so.

BABY TO TORMENTOR: Stop pressuring me. Go away and leave me alone, we have nothing to do with each other. Why shouldn't I stay in here? If I come out I'll just be like you, flailing and empty. . . . My mother wants me out so she can hold me, but that can't last long. (*Voice dim, fading*) I want to stay in here. . . .

TORMENTOR: You can stay in or come out, it makes no difference to me. (*Small laugh*) You're just a blob, something to watch. I don't care about you, I don't even care about your mother. I'm only beating her because she refuses to respond.

FRIEND: You still say these things with a child's voice. Do you really want the mother to respond?

DREAMER: She won't, I know she won't, from the beginning I knew she wouldn't. I guess that's why this whole thing feels so stifling: it's not in anybody's interest to move.

FRIEND: Then let the characters tell each other why it's not in their interest to communicate, why they won't be moved.

TORMENTOR TO MOTHER: You're a very smart lady. (*Big voice*) I guess that's why I'm trying to get you. You know that if you respond—if you kick or bite or scream—you'd start to feel more, and we'd start to feel guilty and want to shut you up and then we'd really have to hurt you, kill you maybe. It's better for the kid and for you not to show any feeling. But the beating goes on because we can't really get our hearts into it when you don't respond, there's no satisfaction, we're just going through motions. It's not really much fun, it's not even pretty, it's not anything. It's just something creepy happening in the corner of a bathroom.

MOTHER TO TORMENTOR: You don't move me. I know you're trying to hook me into your game—your street game—and maybe if I was by myself—if I was empty and bored like you—I would fight back if only to forget the pain. But I have something soft and strong in me and all of you are nothing, you don't even live here. I can be still because I know where I am.

FRIEND: Aha! So the dramatic conflict is between someone who's empty of life and someone who's full of it. Develop those two characters a little.

DREAMER: (*Long silence*) I am full of life. (*Dull voice*) There's something big inside me. It has its own heartbeat.

FRIEND: Be the heartbeat.

DREAMER: (*Irritated at friend*) I don't know how to be a heartbeat. I don't *feel* these things. . . .

FRIEND: You mean you *won't* be a heartbeat?

DREAMER: (*Angry, plaintive*) I don't know what you want from me. You'd like to see me roll around like a baby and admit that I'm just a baby. Well, why should I do that? Why should I admit that I'm a baby? It's enough that I am one.

FRIEND: Pretend that you are me and answer that question.

DREAMER AS FRIEND: Why are you so afraid of being a baby? We all know you need protection, you're soft and mushy, you're mostly heartbeat. Why don't you just accept reality?

FRIEND: Now see if you can allow yourself to be the baby.

DREAMER AS BABY: I hate reality. I am not strong. If I have to be carried I'd rather be alone and in the dark. (*Beginning to weep*) When I was in the womb I was strong; after that it was all downhill. And that's because when I came out *I didn't care,* I didn't believe in anyone else. That's why acting out your dreams is crazy. Life is all acting anyway, so why act about acting? It just proves the absurdity of everything out here. Yeah, I'm an infant; I don't like being alive, it's second rate, just *being here* takes so much work. It would be better to be a rock or a tree, something that didn't have to pretend all the time. That's it: I feel like I have to pretend everything! Pretend to feel, pretend to be different, pretend to be the same, pretend to love, pretend to be happy. Human beings are so pathetic, we spend our whole lives trying to mold things into something else. I'd rather be a simple animal—not the kind that sticks scissors in people—but one that crawls cleanly around on its belly. I popped out of the womb a disappointed old lady and I don't think there's anything to do about it. (*Sobbing*) Inside there's one tiny seed and the rest is just clothing, layers and layers and layers. Jesus! All this energy spent learning how to accept the world we're born into, what could be more unnatural? And how can I ever feel very close to anyone? We start out in the dark and that's the way it stays. I guess all life starts out in a shell or a seed or a root or something, but other animals don't try to pretend, they don't go around beating their chests saying, "We're here and we're so special!" It's all so terrible, and so exhausting. . . .

FRIEND: You've gone all the way into the weak, sad, baby-victim half of your dream. Now see if you can come out and get into the strong, aggressive feelings of power you had as the tormentor. Knock that baby out of her passivity.

DREAMER AS TORMENTOR: Babies aren't human beings, they're just babies. Women exist to have babies, mothers live for babies, babies are the essence of everything. This whole world is a hive of grown-up babies. I don't want to be a baby. I put myself through years of strict training to avoid infancy, why throw it away now? When I die and they do an autopsy they'll see how I ground down my teeth and strained my muscles trying to be an adult and they'll say, "Huh! What a surprise! We thought she was one of us, a real leader. . . ."

FRIEND: Okay, be a leader, a non-baby, a super-adult.

DREAMER AS LEADER: I'm a leader because *I know how to*

make people believe in what nobody believes in. The rest of you are weak, you need me to keep you going because if you stop you'll quit. You must never let down your momentum, never. . . . But good leaders have to be personally believable, so I keep a lot of pressure on myself, I have to stay alert in order to keep the rest of you from losing heart. That's the human-being conspiracy: "If you'll be a leader, we'll be believers." Leaders probably never really believe themselves, which is why they are dependent on their followers.

FRIEND: That's exactly the same split you have in the dream. There are leaders (feelingless people who poke others in order to believe they are alive) and babies (weak, passive creatures who want to be left alone). These two extremes of your personality don't talk to each other, which is why they come out in your dreams. You hurt yourself in order to believe things that are only half real for you, right?

DREAMER: (*Voice soft but clear*) Yeah. I work hard at it. That's the really nightmarish part: *things don't come naturally to me,* you know, easy feelings like it's good, you're good, I'm good, everything's all right, it's a gift to be born. . . . I remember lying in bed at night when I was eleven or twelve, making hard little militant pacts with myself about working harder, being a better leader, not showing any human weaknesses, putting on a better show for the others, rising to the occasion and on and on. . . . I guess the hardest thing in the world for me is to be gentle with myself, to hold myself in my own arms. . . .

THE PLEASURE OF PAIN

What you might do tomorrow depends on whether there is a tomorrow. Some theories of time and personality hold that tomorrow happened yesterday. Others say it is still to come.

Maybe: time is a circle; the future will repeat the past; there is nothing new under the sun; by the time we are five we have been programed so totally that we can never erase the patterns on our brains; freedom is just another word for accepting what is inevitable; change is an illusion; growth is an orderly way of dying; history is a record that plays over and over again. . . .

Or maybe: time is an arrow; the future is open to radically new possibilities; by their actions human beings can create, cause change; freedom is the awful capacity to make the future different from the past; change is always possible; growth is an orderly way of living; history is a path into . . .

The catch is in the maybe. You have at least two possible theories you have to choose between. That means choosing how free you are. You have to decide whether you can decide to change and by your decision you will create one world or another and determine whether tomorrow has already happened.

There is a certain security in thinking that nothing new can happen. It gives confidence that the past provides ready-made models for dealing with every situation; you already have the needles you need with which to knit future experience. If everything is determined life may be a trifle boring ("I have measured out my life with coffee spoons"—T. S. Eliot) but we at least escape the terrors of history. But if the future is open to novelty, tomorrow is an adventure that may turn out better—or worse—than yesterday. Then, like gypsies, our security is in our ability to survive on the open road.

If we are not free to change there is no future to talk about, so let's assume that change is possible, and look at the factors in personality that make it difficult.

When we see ourselves doing the same self-destructive things year after year it's easy to become disillusioned about the possibility of change. Same games. Same mistakes. Why do we sometimes feel perverse pleasure in the pain we cause ourselves by repeating destructive habits?

Masochism is loving the pleasure in pain. It is the clue to why we "rather bear those ills we have than fly to others that we know not of" (Shakespeare, *Hamlet*). We like to think that masochism is limited to perverted personalities, but most of us have at least one room in the mansion of our personality devoted to self-torture. Consider the mental anguish involved in small worries, anxieties, continual self-doubts; in the slow suicide of chronic anger or depression; in addiction to work, the more righteous sacrifice made on the altar of the "bitch-goddess, Success" (William James). Perhaps the majority of human suffering is self-imposed.

A story from Charles Lamb gives a clue to the mystery of self-imposed pain. Once upon a time in ancient China a house burned down, with a pig inside. While poking around the ashes the villagers came upon the roasted pig and began to sample this new delicacy. Captivated by the delicious taste, they got another pig, put it in another house, and set that house afire. Early in life we learn that pleasure accompanies otherwise destructive or painful conduct. When we are sick, we are rewarded with attention; when we by-pass pleasure for duty, we are praised; when we are docile and obedient, we are loved. We learn early that the betrayal of our inner feelings and desires is often the price of social acceptance. Change happens once we learn that it is possible to have roast pig without burning down a house. Pleasure is a gift that doesn't necessarily depend on sacrifice.

It takes courage to admit that we have created much of our suffering, and to take steps to dismiss it. Strength and tenderness are needed for us to tolerate happiness.

VIEWPOINTS

The pleasure we get from suffering is one of our most carefully guarded secrets. We like to deny the pay-offs of pain. Like Prometheus, we blame the gods and ignore our complicity in creating our fate. See what happens when you reverse your story and take total responsibility for your sorrows.

> * In what ways do you repeat (year after year) patterns that are frustrating to you? Describe the circles.
> * Imagine yourself at your worst. How do you use this weak, suffering, helpless self to get your way with other persons? (Do you collect nobility points for constant striving? Martyr points for doing distasteful duty? Poor-little-me points for being sick?)
> * Tell about the sorrowful, tragic battles of your soul in a way that will make your audience laugh instead of cry.

Here are some clues to help you reverse your story.

> * Sick people are powerful. They make the healthy feel guilty.
> * The fears of the weak and fragile establish the limits of any relationship. The meek inherit the earth by sapping the energies of the bold.
> * Victims enjoy the luxury of saying, "I can't." When you were young you got punished if you said, "I won't," and helped if you said, "I can't."

Someday My Prince Will Come

My visions about my life have always been so grand that any change of direction is a major undertaking. The first big leap I ever made was leaving Europe during the First World

War. I was still a young girl, the oldest of five children. Things in Vienna did not look good for us, so I quit my job, took a boat to America, found work, and sent for my brothers and sister. My sister died but now, fifty years later, the boys are still with me.

I grew up steeped in German romanticism, so naturally I had grand fantasies about passionate love and adventure, finding my prince and walking with him into eternity. But first I had to settle the family and make certain that we would be financially secure. A certain gentleman helped me set up shop here and then took financial advantage of me. I was horribly shocked! How could a nice, elderly man do that to a young girl? After that I was careful never to trust anyone in matters of money.

I taught my brothers to be hairdressers and married a man who gave me security though he was not my prince. We were divorced after thirty years, but in the meantime I bought some property on a hill in California and moved the whole family (the boys and my own two children) up there. All of them expected me to be the Rock of Gibraltar, and I didn't let them down. I was still privately waiting for my Only Beloved, but meanwhile the duties of the blood took priority over longings of the flesh. Year after year I watched over everything. In fact, I played my cards so well that eventually I was virtually invulnerable to outside forces. I've always been broad-minded—all sorts of people pass through my life—but my self-control protected me from contamination. No one could take advantage of me because I stuck to my own affairs; understand what I mean? My family and I were never invaded.

All those years while I plotted a safe course I told myself that this is the way we Jews had to do in order not to be invaded by wrong ideas and materialism and sex indulgence.

The family stayed together (we all still live on this hill), the children stayed close to home, the property tripled in value, the community knew who we were. But when I was sixty I stepped down from my pedestal long enough to see the price I'd paid: my prince had never come. The romantic dream of one-to-one union was dead. Seeking to have and give security had bought me such invulnerability that there was no prince around passionate enough to wake up Snow White. After sixty years I saw that the Rock of Gibraltar was a hunk of stone.

It was a mistake to think that security and passion could exist in the same applecart. One upsets the other! I hated to let go of that dream, but passion is too ephemeral, too deceptive; everybody knows it burns you out and brings early death. If you become one of the masses you are lost. And if you are lost, prosperity can't find you. The great passions are a thing of the past, I decided. What I wanted was to rise above romance and fleshly appetites, to be independent, even of God. . . .

So for twelve years I've been endeavoring to recast my romantic dream in spiritual terms, something more appropriate to my age. Now the men I fall in love with are gurus, men with a spiritual fire in their souls to whom I can respond from a distance. Zorba always dies, but the realm of Gurdjieff and Meher Baba lives on eternally. When death comes for you the body disintegrates but the soul survives: there are no limits to one's possibilities after death.

But sometimes I fear that I've gone too far, that I can no more abandon myself to spiritual rapture than I could to romantic passion. . . . I don't know, there's still time, maybe another way will come to me. . . .

In fact, just last night I dreamed that as I was stepping into the bathtub a strange woman appeared and said, "Why are you bathing here? The water is full of blood." I said, "But

why shouldn't I bathe in it? It's my own blood!" She led me
into the living room and pointed to a square, sunken tub in
the center of the floor full of clear water. She suggested that I
bathe in there. "In front of everybody?" I protested. "All the
rest of the family bathes in the bathroom, I've always done
it that way, why shouldn't I go on?" When I woke up I felt
that maybe the woman was suggesting a new, unstructured
path for me. Maybe now I am to come down to the ground
where everyone else is, bathe in public, expose myself in front
of everyone, become vulnerable—the one thing I've always
dreaded. Maybe sinking down is actually the other side of
the path to enlightenment! Even talking this way feels like
some kind of preparation for death, returning to the earth
what belongs to the earth. But if I let go of my controls, I'd
run around madly embracing everybody, and then wouldn't
I lose my uniqueness, my soul? It's so terribly difficult to know
for sure. . . .

PLANNING TO BE HUMAN

Plans are dangerous necessities. If we plan too much, we're
always living ahead of ourselves, rehearsing scenes that usually
don't happen. We can spend a lifetime paying for insurance
against catastrophes that never materialize. Those who live in
the future miss many of the pleasures of the present. But if we
refuse to plan at all, there are some kinds of fulfillment we
miss. Many of the most beautiful flowers bloom only when
carefully fertilized and cultivated; art involves discipline;
learning guitar or gourmet cooking requires an investment of
energy over a period of time.

Something in each of us resists making decisions and plans.

When the imagination is soaring each decision feels like a forced landing, a little death. But when we act we strengthen our self-definition and gain personal power.

Decisions dealing with self-change may be creative or destructive. A shade too much pressure and our ideals can turn into whiplike demands. Will-power (the revolutionary minority in the psyche) dictates to the entire body how life and personality are to be structured. Heavy-handed dictators provoke repression and rebellion. Won't-power always counters will-power; those aspects of the personality that don't fit into a five-year-ideal-self plan resist the dictates of the will. The result is schizophrenia, civil war.

When there's a gun at your head, it's tough to relax and let change occur. Psychological and political growth toward a more harmonious state usually happens naturally when self-acceptance is high and the pressure for change is gentle. That's when dry decisions can flower into creative choice.

VIEWPOINTS

Keep one eye on what dissatisfies you about yourself now, and it is easier to design a satisfying future. Imagine that you have a fatal disease and have one month left to live.

> * What do you still want to do? How will you spend the month of life that remains to you? (Give yourself full energy, plenty of money, and freedom from pain until the end.)
> * What will be the epitaph on your tombstone?

Good news—you've just been granted a reprieve. You have a long time to live—ten, twenty, seventy years, who knows. . . . What will you do with your time?

* Draw a floor plan of a house you would like to be living in ten years hence. Who lives with you? What are the physical surroundings like? What is the mood of the place?
* How do you spend your time inside and outside the house? With whom? What is your work?
* What feelings do you experience that were strange to you ten years ago?
* When you have done this fantasy put it aside and do it another way. Give yourself a variety of alternative futures to move around in.

Fantasies are loaded because they put us in touch with our repressed or unrealized desires. Once a desire becomes conscious it demands some kind of response. If we don't say yes or no to specific fantasies, frustration can immobilize us. Move from fantasy to decision. Pick one of the desires uncovered in your exploration of dreams and fantasies and commit yourself to taking the first steps toward its realization. Plan some future action that will positively alter the external or internal world in which you live.

If I had a month to live I would:

* Ask my doctor for the name and address of someone who had *two* months to live so that at last I could be relevant to the rest of someone else's life
* Try to talk a record company into buying my guaranteed Buddy Holly-type interrupted success story (cf. Janis Joplin, Jimi Hendrix, messages beyond the grave . . .)
* Rape Gayle Tawny. As Iago said in *Othello:* Why kill yourself for the love of a woman when you can rape her and be publicly hanged, thus satisfying both desires?
* Ask my friend the cameraman to film my death as I beat Evel Knievel to the act of jumping across the Grand Canyon

 * Consider hijacking a plane and dropping money over Glastonbury, Connecticut
 * Weigh the benefits of political assassination

If I had a month to live I would:

 * Not tell anyone
 * Try to make every moment meaningful
 * Pace myself in such a way that I could accomplish more
 * Spend more time in spiritual growth
 * Pray and meditate more for good karma
 * Give away all my personal belongings to people who would need and appreciate them
 * Arrange for my own cremation
 * Tell all my friends and family how much I love them

If I had a month to live I would:

 * Invite everyone around here to a party
 * Give everything I own away to the guests
 * Stock up on necessary drugs
 * Buy a super high fidelity tape deck (portable) and a very good motion picture camera with plenty of film
 * Arrange for someone to retrieve the full tapes and films after I'm gone

If I had a month to live I would:

 * Make love a lot
 * Enjoy my children! Listen beneath their words to the world they live in. Tape-record some things I would like to have told them when they were older.
 * Eat and talk with friends, and visit my mother, brother, and sisters
 * Fly to Paris and spend several days in the most luxurious

hotel there and buy expensive presents for all my friends
and charge them to my American Express credit card
(sorry, the deceased left no forwarding address)
* Fly to the most remote South Sea island I could find and
spend several days with nothing but sun and sea
* Come home and spend my last days among familiar
things preparing for the unfamiliar thing
* (I would like *not* to write a little book on the last month
of life, though I probably would)

If I had a month to live I would:

   * Go on working, as always

VI

COSMIC TIME

Transcending Here and Now

The dates on the tombstone—John Doe 1937–2009—mark the outer limits of a single life; seventy-two years in Illinois. That's all there is for John.

Or is it? Sometimes a crack opens in time and we wonder whether there are other ways of timing and spacing our lives:

"The dream was especially vivid. I knew someone had drowned while skin diving and I had to search for the body. I put on an aqualung and went to the bottom of the narrow channel of water. I found nothing. Suddenly I was swept away by a current. I knew I would be drowned. But I wasn't. In the next scene I was explaining to the military officer in charge of the search for the body how I had miraculously escaped death. . . . I was so shaken by the dream I got up and wrote it down. Five or six hours later I received news that a close friend of mine just drowned while skin diving off the coast of Maine."

If mind is encapsulated in body, how can it travel in time and space?

There are enough accounts of clairvoyance, ESP, and mystical awareness to make any reasonable person question the dogma that says we are all complete captives of clock time and geographical space. The question is not whether we can transcend sequential time but in what ways we do so. Religious persons speak of atemporal experiences as vistas opening to God, Spirit, Universal Mind, the Void, or the Cosmos. Others consider them subjective states of mind, an "oceanic feeling" (Freud), or a state of psychedelic awareness.

We are in the middle of a consciousness revolution in which orthodox religion and traditional science are being over thrown. For many people God is truly dead. The formal practices of religion do not, for many people, produce transcendence. There is also a weariness with the closed push-pull universe of popular science. Widespread experimentation with techniques for transcendence (drugs, meditation, yoga, Sufi exercises, divination, astrology, Zen) reflects our desire to recapture a magical sense of the openness of the cosmos. We want out of the impersonal, anonymous universe where everything can be explained by the laws of cause and effect and probability. We long to regain the primitive feeling that nature has some kindly, even motherly intent toward her human creations. And why deny that some force at least as intelligent as an IBM computer (and perhaps more tender) might be responsible for morning glories and the insatiable human appetite for significance?

A free person is a cognitive outlaw, one who rejects official ideologies and interprets experience with homemade categories. In considering what journeys may be taken in and out of ordinary time it helps to stick close to raw experience and avoid the packaged explanations and language of religion, psychology, or science.

THE TWO-FACED WORLD

It seems as if the world was designed, or not designed, to drive us mad. We think we recognize order but then chaos makes it all absurd. Reality is schizophrenic; order and accident, design and chance are locked in eternal battle.

Most of the time the universe appears to be governed by rational powers. Things usually happen according to the rules. The tides follow mathematically calculable patterns. Acorns regularly grow into oak trees, not persimmons. When we see the starry skies above we secretly suspect (as Immanuel Kant argued) that some provident God designed the world. Things seem to fit together (men and women). Causes and effects were made for each other. The evidence suggests (*almost* beyond reasonable doubt) that reason governs reality.

Most cultures have assumed that some divine mind or minds are homogenized with nature and that it's possible to harmonize human life with the will of God, with the Tao, with the force that draws the pine trees toward the sun, with the laws of nature. The Greeks contemplated the stars and thought they could pattern their politics and ethics on the divine regularities that ruled the heavens. With less reverence but equal hope we use space probes and computers to track down the hidden logic in things. And we trust that one day our sacred science will dispel the mystery and reveal the predictable order that lies beneath apparent chance.

But just when we are about to pronounce the universe sane it shows its other face. We expect the usual thing to happen and along comes a snowstorm in August, a deformed child, or a duck-billed platypus. Chance and accident seem to be stronger than law and order. And, worst of all, the wrong people die young. There is no moral or logical reason why a child should die of leukemia. When some misfit makes an impossible shot and kills our President, it's hard to escape the impression that some indifferent God is playing bingo with the universe.

The arbitrariness of things is enough to give anyone who thinks about it a case of existential anxiety or a taste for superstition and magical rituals. Lady Luck's a fickle bitch and it's hard to figure out how she operates, yet some people definitely have the knack for walking out of accidents and picking horses. Maybe luck is nothing more than being open to whatever happens and avoiding the illusion that reason rules. Lucky people know the world is magical so they're not surprised by accidents; like children and drunks, they relax when they fall. And who is to say that magic is irrational? If everything is disjointed a black cat may be more predictive of the future than computerized trends. Why not cut the deck, or read Tarot cards, or consult fortune cookies? Maybe these are precisely the liturgies that win the favor of Lady Luck.

It is no wonder that many of us are a little confused. To survive in the world we have to learn how and when to use reason or intuition, investigation or divination, logic or magic. At best, there is never enough order in things to satisfy our appetite for harmony. But neither is chaos consistent enough to destroy our fascination with reason. After you've done everything you can think of, it never hurts to cross your fingers.

VIEWPOINTS

Religion has been used as a tuning fork to adjust the vibrations of an individual life to the rhythms of the cosmos. Whether we use meditation, dice, prayer, daisy petals, or astrology, each of us has some way of keeping in touch with the governing rhythms of the world.

* How do you stay together with the basic rhythms of your psyche and nature?
* What cycles do you experience in your body that are responsive to the moon or the seasons?
* What do you do when you are out of sync, when everything's going wrong, when you get up on the wrong side of the bed, when you can't get it together?

Although we can't defend our superstitions rationally, most of us practice some magical rituals to court good luck and ward off evil.

* What lucky objects protect you against the irrationality of the world? (A rabbit's foot, four-leaf clover, St. Christopher medal, a favorite shirt?) Do you depend on them? What would you do if you lost one of them?
* When you have to make decisions and the alternatives seem evenly balanced, what do you do? (Flip a coin and do the opposite, cast the I Ching, visit your psychiatrist, pray, consult the stars?)
* What rituals do you have for warding off bad luck? (Crossing yourself, knocking on wood, throwing salt over your shoulder?)

The Old Oak

When I lose my path I have certain ways of finding it
again. Sometimes I take a large sheet of paper and make a list
of beautiful scenes. They always have to do with my childhood: something about the ocean, or dark Florida nights
when the stars hang down so you feel you can reach up and
pluck them.

When I turn to my oak tree I'm desperate. It's a huge creature, standing eternally in the back yard of the house where I
was born and grew up. In the fall of the year when the storms
came up from the Caribbean I would stand at the window
of the house watching and listening to the limbs of the peach
trees and the persimmons and sometimes the big bay trees
snapping under the wind. And then I'd watch the oak tree,
and the only thing it did was sway ever so slightly all in one
piece, not even dropping a leaf.

So the oak tree and I reached an understanding. As a child
when I had problems I couldn't handle (the kind when you
envision yourself in your coffin, and the weeping mother at
the graveside, and how sorry they all are that they've done
this thing to you), I would think of my tree. No matter what
my problem was, if I could get to my oak tree and sit down
and lean against it and feel it on my back, then I knew that I
could tell my whole sadness and be contained. I worked out
all my religious problems under that oak tree. When I couldn't
understand what they were saying in church about Jesus I
would sit down there and talk it all out. The oak and Jesus
became all mixed up together. I felt such a personal com-
panionship with them that I never had any theological problem about Jesus as the Son of God. It's the same way for me

now. Any time I feel sad or at a loss, I beat a path, in my mind, back to the old oak.

Like the Time I Filled a Bag with Apples and Climbed on a Horse to Ride Off Forever

One morning I got up with the sun and felt one of those brilliant crystal days coming on. So my friend David and I threw together some apples and almonds and cider and whizzed through the city to get to the country.

David's place was a Quonset hut in the middle of nowhere with cottonwood trees out front, a couple of horses standing around, an old windmill, and a half-finished geodesic dome. We walked around, visiting the windmill and listening to it squeak, talking to the horses, climbing the dome. After a while I took off all my clothes (except for my boots), tied them around me, and walked off across the hills.

It was a relief to be off the highway, out where you could see things from 360 degrees. I was clumping through the bushes, feeling the depth of things, my feet contacting the earth step by step, entranced by the glitter in the rocks, nothing on my mind except my movement. I was following a cowpath along a fence line and eventually found myself making a large circle. I could hear the horses nickering and tromping around, and I wanted to ride.

One of the horses was an old brood mare with a strange look in her eye; the other one was very young. I wondered if he was her colt, but when I went up and spoke to him I realized that the two of them were simply friends and it would be all right to ride him. Right away I looked around for a rope to fix a bridle but I couldn't find a thing. I kept stumbling over wires and cans and started feeling frustrated. Finally I decided to use a piece of soft wire, but as I was yanking it down from the tin roof I tripped over the perfect piece of rope, curled neatly at my feet. The pleasant surprise rocked me back into slow motion. I put the wire back where it came from and fitted a bridle to the horse.

Then I went to the truck, took out a white paper bag, and started filling it with apples. As I was doing this I got the idea that I was packing for a little longer trip than just across the fields and back, and the fantasy grew in a great rush: I would just go away, leaving the angular part of the world far behind me! As I filled up the bag I felt tremendously excited, thinking about the canyons and sunlight and mist, and me riding off forever.

So I got on the horse, all set to go with a jug in one hand and a bag of apples in the other, and then the horse swung his head around and bit a hole in the bottom of my bag! Everything fell out, apples bumping all over the roadway. I just sat there for a moment. Then I got down and started gathering while the horse munched away on a bright red apple.

The horse bit a hole in my flight plans and brought me to earth in one big bump. He was telling me: not so fast, riding off forever throws everything off balance, this is as far as you have to go today! I climbed back on to see where he was going and we traveled about twenty feet before he stopped cold. I got off, put the rope down, and walked back, laughing at the wonder of it all.

That was a day! Everything fit together in such a perfect circle: speeding along the freeway to get away, feeling the organic beauty of the countryside; getting tangled in the wires of my big plans; the ideal rope appearing at my feet; deciding to ride off forever; the horse showing me I wasn't ready; and then that cascade of bouncing apples. . . . In the silence I could see the folly of trying to force my trip on natural rhythms, trying to blend into the mist and evaporate. The nice thing was that I also recognized the beauty of the true images: the earth, my feet, the sun, the horse, a bag of apples. Everything was there for me. All I had to do was respond.

MIRACLES, MAGIC, AND SYNCHRONICITY

"I hadn't seen Jane for years but her occasional letters were filled with echoes of darkness. I thought about her often. So when I was in California on business I planned to visit her, but I didn't call ahead of time. The day before I returned home I was driving through the town where she lived and stopped at a roadside phone booth to call her. There was no answer. I left the booth and walked to a nearby gas station to use the men's room. When I came there was Jane with a flat tire. A coincidence? What does that mean? Though we didn't know what to name the forces that brought us together, we both knew the meeting had been arranged."

Whether the world is intimate or impersonal, lawful or magical depends on your perspective. World views are like glasses: they can be steel gray, rosy, or black and white. In the matter of cosmic sight we all wear some kind of lenses.

Children and primitive peoples live in a personalized universe. They experience events as tailor-made to match their needs. Omens, signs, and miracles flash forth from every tree and hilltop: bushes burn and are not consumed; birds bring messages from the gods; among the Bushmen of Africa the stars (kinfolk of an earlier race now dwelling in the sky) guide the aim of the hunter; the Hopi snake dance brings summer rains. In childhood we all live at the enchanted center of things. We know that chairs trip us when we're angry; we move through the forest and the thicket opens automatically. The world is a conspiracy contrived to delight us.

But once we become mature we put away childish notions of magic, abandon the egocentric perspective, and learn to observe the world with neutral eyes. We are encouraged to filter out the voices that address us in the wind and rain, close off supernatural whisperings in dreams, and become citizens of a universe that is unresponsive to intuitions. We adopt a skepticism that becomes the foundation of what we narrowly identify as reason.

Fortunately, our sophistication does not prevent the world from going its magical way. Things keep happening that jolt our minds; events bend themselves to fit our private needs; hunches pan out; clairvoyant moments burst into daylight consciousness; prophetic dreams visit us in spite of our skepticism; happy accidents, coincidences, or synchronicities are as common as breath.

VIEWPOINTS

Our psyches have an automatic mechanism for shaking off weird experiences which disturb our normal ways of understanding. For years mainstream scientists have been reluctant to admit the existence of UFOs, extrasensory perception or clairvoyance because they couldn't explain them. Sort through your experiences and bring out the bizarre, marvelous, and inexplicable.

* What fortunate accidents, coincidences, synchronicities, or lucky breaks have befallen you?
* What events seem prearranged?

* What premonitions have you had of future events?
(Prophetic dreams? Hunches?)
* Describe trances or communications from other people
you have received. From the dead?
* What evidence could you collect to support the hypoth-
esis that you are at the center of a world which was
planned for you and is responsive to you?

Dear St. Anthony

My life is studded with miracles, like two-cent sequins. I
stay in circulation so magic has lots of chances to find me.
As a kid I walked around crossing myself and chanting:
"Something's lost and can't be found, dear St. Anthony,
look around." And I found things: money, medallions, caps,
comic books, old photos, everything! One afternoon last
month I showed up in San Francisco and went to Lilac Street
where an old friend of mine was staying. I didn't know her
house number so I walked up and down the four blocks of Lilac until I found the house that felt right—a big Victorian
thing with lots of units and porches and clotheslines. I went
upstairs and knocked on number 7. Nancy opened the door
with a kid in her arms. She was at a neighbor's house
baby-sitting for a couple of hours, and she was amazed to see
me. . . .

I love pictures. I also like to drop spare change into pot-
luck machines looking for omens. One day I fed a machine at
the beach arcade and won some playing cards with pictures
of Hollywood cowboys painted on them: Gene Autry, king of
diamonds; Roy Rogers, jack of hearts; Fred MacMurray, ten
of spades. I put them in my pocket and carried them around
with me. A few days later a friend of mine was in a funk and I
said, "Here, Alec, I have something for you," and handed

him the Fred MacMurray card. It worked like a charm; it spun his head around: it turns out that Fred MacMurray was his Boy Scout master!

Magic or divination or synchronicity is simply making connection with real chemical/electrical bonds of some sort that aren't picked up if you're moving too fast or not looking out for them. The night my father died in Central Islip Mental Hospital four out of his six kids received messages from him. He died between two and four in the morning. Mary, asleep in a ski lodge in Vermont, had a nightmare in which her husband chopped Pop to death with an ax. Kay, who sleeps like Rip Van Winkle woke unexplainably at two and couldn't get back to sleep for several hours. I was at home getting high with some friends when suddenly, about 1 A.M., I fell into an airless despair. It was so complete that I didn't even try to understand but lay down on the floor and floated in it. At about two it lifted off as fast as it came, so I got up and went right back to talking. My sister called the next morning to say the old man was dead. My brother showed up soon after, and when I told him he said, "I knew it! I woke Pamela up in the night to tell her the old man croaked in my dream!" Our father was a madman, but his madness was rooted in common magic: his death was electric with it.

Here Is There and Then Is Now

Ten years ago I was convinced that there was nothing psychic about me. But as I went deeper into yoga and meditation and Edgar Cayce's books I began to wonder.

One day I went with a friend to a class in psychic development and ended up enrolling. The teacher was a medium who would sometimes fall into trances and strange voices

would speak through her, a thing which later happened to
a few other members of the class. It was there that I first
heard of psychometry. The teacher explained that people
leave vibrations on objects that they own or hold for any
length of time, and a sensitive is often able to know things
about the person's past lives by holding the item and con-
centrating. At first I didn't like psychometry, I didn't see
how I could possibly distinguish between the fantasies of my
own vivid imagination and a true reading. Then one day I
was meditating at a Quaker meeting and feeling deeply
peaceful when quite unexpectedly I experienced myself as
somebody else. I was sitting there dressed in long dark clothes
surrounded by four children, obviously mine. There was a
bonnet on my head and I knew my name, Hannah, Hannah
Whitfield or Whitcomb—I wasn't quite sure. At that moment
I was engulfed by a deep, anguished feeling of bereavement.
I knew that my husband had just been buried; he'd been
chopping wood and the ax had glanced off a knot in the log
and gone into his left leg, causing death by infection. I sat
promising myself and his memory that somehow I'd bring
up our children properly by myself.

It all happened in a flash. Even as I was saying to myself,
"Wow, what an imagination!" I somehow knew it was
nothing of the sort. My imagination just isn't that good, so
many details, so fast, so undirected. Could I have tuned
into some earlier life?

Nothing else like that happened for a few months until I
began giving yoga lessons to my friend Lee at her house in the
country. Lee is one of the most psychic people I've ever
known. The two of us started playing with the Ouija board
and we began to get interesting messages from the other
side. Soon her friend Ed joined us. We sat at the board every
week, and my life took on a new excitement that hasn't left

it since. We began to see bits and pieces of our past lives fitting together. In one of them I was married to Ed, and a slender handsome man named Ernšt was my lover. One day Ernst spoke through the board, asking to be my spiritual guide. When I accepted (a bit dubiously) the pointer looped and figure-eighted all over the board with his rejoicing, and my life was changed forever.

After that other visions from past lives would pop into my mind when I meditated. It was quite unlike ordinary thinking; more like when you've been trying hard to remember a name and as soon as you give up it pops bright and clear into your mind. Often these memories come flooded with associated emotion. For instance, I remember one day emerging from meditation sobbing over the vision of Ernst being gored to death by a bull that had surprised us while we were making love in a field in sixteenth-century Belgium.

As my psychic life opened up, my gift for psychometry grew too, and I worked with other people more and more. Holding an object between my palms, I would sit quietly with my eyes closed and my mind as still as I could hold it. I'd give a silent prayer for protection and guidance and turn inward for the other person. I was astonished at the variety of pictures that unfolded, sometimes in considerable detail. I found that if I asked a question silently such as, "What country?" or "What century?" I would somehow usually know the answer. I could work only a short time, however, before the pictures became dim or I started feeling my imagination taking over and had to stop. If I was very tired nothing happened at all.

Early on I looked into the lives of a particularly gentle girl and saw her as a Scythian chieftain, returning to the battlefield after a battle with the Greeks. He was searching for his young son who had gone into battle by his side. I hesitated there, as I didn't know who the Scythians were or if they'd ever fought the Greeks (later research proved that they had), but the scene led me on. I watched the chieftain heaving aside several bloody corpses and uncovering the mutilated body of his son. I don't know if I shared his revulsion or whether it was just my own I was feeling, but I felt such a wave of nausea that I nearly gagged, throwing the ring back at its owner. It was ten minutes before I was normal again. I realized that the warrior's soul lesson had been so violent that this gentle person had never again returned in a male body.

Another time I saw a girl as a native woman in Brazil. She had carelessly left her young child playing by the river and she and I watched in helpless horror as the great jaws of a crocodile closed on one round leg and dragged him screaming under water. I handed back her article, saying I believed that the little boy had returned in this life as her three-year-old son. She stared at me in wonder. "You couldn't have known," she said, "but lately he's been afraid of the dark. He has the idea that there's a crocodile in his room trying to eat him up!"

I was as awed as she was. It's very hard to shake the suspicion that you're making everything up out of whole cloth. Again and again I've had verification, and yet I'm always surprised because I always suspect myself. Every time I begin a reading I explain to the person that I have no idea if what I recount is the truth or not, that they alone can know, because it is their soul memory that I'm trying to pipe into, and the knowledge is buried in their subconscious.

Ernst, my guide from the other world, explained to us that we're working with a natural energy which is as real as electricity or television. "Actually, it's more like radio than anything else," he told us. "Some days you can get a far-off station clearly and yet another day the same tuning gives you nothing but gobbledygook. Someday the scientific world will recognize psychometry and be able to control it as they do radio."

I wonder what will happen next! Now I'm much more available and vulnerable to good and evil powers than most people are. But I'm not afraid, I'm "on the path," so my life is filled with joy and purpose. I used to be afraid of the dark, but now when I'm alone the darkness is filled with friends! Getting in touch with past lives helps me to understand the contradictions in myself and in others. I see that we will all return for other lives and other lessons in the future: death is a door, but I'm in no hurry to go through it. Life is exciting, and afterward Ernst and I can be together. He tries to explain that here is there and then is now, but that's a little too much for me to comprehend. "Just you be there when I finish my work here and come over," I tell him. "Don't you worry!" he answers, waltzing joyously around the Ouija board.

PARADISE: Lost and Found

Once upon a time we were all natives of paradise. Some say it was a garden of delight; some say it was a gold-paved city luminous with justice and good will. At the very least it was a state of unbroken pleasure.

But something happened. The serpent entered; paradise vanished; primeval childhood ended; ego ate id; the bourgeoisie gained control of the means of production and exploited the working class; separation anxiety led us to possess the world and make it safe by work; the pain of parental rejection numbed our nerve endings and our wonder.

It is widely agreed that alienation is the condition of man but there is no agreement about how he fell from grace. From a psychological point of view the process is easily described. Early in the socialization process a child learns that he can get love only if he denies desire and obeys parents and other big people. Thus he develops a split—a polite schizophrenia for nice people—between private feeling and public action. The child learns—is taught—to be a double agent. His private world is a paradise where the pleasure principle governs; to survive he becomes a naturalized citizen of the adult world governed by the reality principle. Every child knows when he consents to citizenship in the real world that he is betraying paradise. In time he adjusts; only infrequently do remembrances of happiness trouble his righteousness.

But periodic pleasure creates a hunger for more. Some fools and some heroes insist that if paradise has been lost it can be regained. Wise men warn us that this may be an illusion. They counsel us to accept the necessity of alienation: better to settle for civilization and its discontents than to dream of paradise and wake up cold, hungry, afraid, angry, lost, and disillusioned. Freud told us: work and love; the world is too dangerous for children.

Whether or not we can ever create a society of the un-alienated, we can at least lessen the alienation in ourselves. Every person has traces of paradise inside. If we once locate our feelings of harmony we can learn to move in and out of them almost at will. Memories of primal pleasure are alive and well in the unconscious; all we need to do is call them forth.

VIEWPOINTS

To remember the fall is to move a step closer to paradise. Beneath primal pain lies primal pleasure; we only hate those we loved; the apple was even more delicious before it became a forbidden fruit.

    * When did you fall from grace, lose your ease?
    * When do you first remember lying? Being ashamed? Hiding? Feeling small and inadequate? When did you get your second face?
    * When did you discover the limitations in your mother? Best friend? A hero?

Allow your thoughts to float back to the most ecstatic times of childhood. Remember how your body felt when you could run tirelessly, when there was no tomorrow or yesterday, when everything in the world was just right, when you felt loved and secure and free. Try to recapture specific scenes.

    * What keeps you out of the garden now?
    * A Hypothesis: the hard realism of adult consciousness is abnormal and the childhood state of appreciation is the natural state of awareness. Now what?

Solitary Confinement

I don't know exactly how I fell from grace, but I definitely knew when I was down. Thud. It had something to do with slipping out of my mother's lap when she would gladly have rocked me and held me longer: I was three years old and had no time for baby stuff. I was too busy rushing after my older sister and brother, hustling to keep them from noticing that I had a little trouble walking, running, climbing, spelling, and reading at their speed. More than comfort, I wanted the big time.

So suddenly I wasn't a child any more but a small double agent, consciously conning a world that wasn't mine. Since I was my only confidant I would plan and scheme and talk to myself when I was alone. My fall from innocence was literal. I bit into consciousness and then *it* began to eat *me*.

I started collecting things, hoarding. Boxes of banana Popsicles hidden in the basement freezer under loaves of Wonder Bread. My diary full of petty confessions. And money. I remember those horrid, breezeless summer afternoons when I'd close myself in my room, dig my alligator-skin squeeze-purse out of my rainboots, pour the coins on the bed, and start counting. Oh, it was a miserable ritual! With the door bolted no one ever interrupted me, but at the same time I was trapped in there. My careful private accounting system kept me safe and captive.

Now I try to avoid that airless six-year-old's room whenever I have the choice. It feels like a death trap. I try to stay outside, keep moving, visit friends on their turf, but sometimes I fall into states of mind that have the same sticky, suffocating feeling of that other room, and then, instantly, I am a prisoner. Since I don't trust anyone to come in there with me (aren't two immobilized twice as miserable as one?) I go in there utterly alone, resigned to do my time as intensely as I can to get it over with. Sometimes I manage to dig my way out, but otherwise I only hope to finish out my sentence.

GOOD AND EVIL—AND BEYOND

Go(o)d and (D)evil depend on each other like concave and convex. The same instinct in us that personifies good into God transforms evil into Devil. We put human faces on good and evil to try to humanize the universe. God created man in His image and man returned the favor. One of the reasons we create gods and angels is because we want to believe that the world is ruled by benevolent powers. But when these powers do not eliminate suffering, tragedy, and death we evoke a panoply of devils, witches, and monsters to absorb the blame for evil.

Because gods and goddesses do not die they reassure us that something abides; beyond our time and space there is a reality invulnerable to death; the Rock of Ages is not washed away by the river. The logic of religion is reflected in the primitive practice of driving an *axis mundi*—a world-pole—into the ground at the place where a mystic, shaman, or priest has received a vision or revelation of God. The tribe, then, organizes its life around this point—the sacred center of the world. All lines radiate from the church steeple (or the Capitol building); the holy is the centering point for human life, the firm foundation, the Eternal Rock. Paul Tillich translated this religious act into psychological language when he said that whatever concerns us ultimately is our God. Even if "God is dead" the presence of the holy permeates the place where our needs for security and meaning are met. Whatever passion is at the center of our lives—work, money, family, music, education, baseball, romance—promises salvation and demands ultimate loyalty.

The Devil is still with us. The forces of evil are organized and, consciously or unconsciously, they conspire against us. They are out to get us: The Establishment, Whitey, Male Chauvinist Pigs, Capitalist Pigs, Dirty Hippies, Atheistic Commies, Niggers, the FBI. Or (for psychological sophisticates who don't believe in projection or the Devil) evil is reduced to abstract qualities within the self: fear, hostility, passivity, repression, primal pain, or weak will.

Regardless of what we call them, our modern dualisms divide us as much as the old ones did: whether we project Good and Evil outward on God and the Devil or inward on Eros and Aggression the split remains. And a split world means a perpetual battleground between the white and the black, a habitat for schizophrenics. The effort to root out the evil we create by our definitions spreads the disease. In the long run our best solution is to proclaim an armistice, an end to dualism, and welcome the warring factions into the human commonwealth. The opposites belong together, the contradictions can be encompassed. The Devil is Lucifer, God's fallen angel; Eros waits under Aggression; strength is hidden just below the fault in personality. An old Eastern proverb sums it up: "Where you stumble and fall there you will find the gold." Nietzsche pointed the way toward the unity of personality when he challenged us to go "beyond good and evil." We can trust life to break through our brittle moral judgments and rise up like a seedling from the husks of its old confines.

VIEWPOINTS

Even if we have no official organizational chart we all have a private demonology. (To whom does your Secretary of Greed

report? Do you have separate ministries for the Seven Deadly
Sins?) What demons, devils, ghouls, witches, evil spirits, monsters (or shadows, frustrations, fears, inhibitions, repressions,
and complexes) make up your private underworld?

    * How is your hell organized? Draw a map, make a chart,
or compile a catalogue of personnel.
    * As Commander-in-Chief of the Forces of Light, how do
you combat the Powers of Darkness? What evil do you
wage war against? How?
    * As the Prince of Darkness, how do you undermine the
Forces of Light?
    * The bad guys should get what's coming to them. In your
hell how are offenders punished? What is the appropriate
punishment? Reward?

If this were the best of all possible worlds we might love
mystery more and explanations less. But since evil shatters our
security we tell stories to explain why a world that is so intri-
cate and marvelous misses perfection by the shadow of a
tragedy. All people create a myth to explain why evil exists:
because Satan rebelled against God, or because spirit and
matter are incompatible, or because the cosmic consciousness is
not yet fully awakened, or because the bourgeoisie exploits
the proletariat, or . . .

    * Make up your own myth. Why are there pain and malev-
olence in the world? Is there an end to evil?

The Greeks personified their ultimate concerns by creating
a pantheon of gods and goddesses: Aphrodite, goddess of
love; Pan, god of wild things; Athena, goddess of the polis;
Zeus, ruler of Olympus . . . Describe the pantheon of the
gods that move you. Give names and faces to the concerns
at the center of your life.

The Leer of the Monkey Devil

A few years back I woke up in the middle of the night filled with a vast terror. I hadn't been dreaming and couldn't explain my sudden fright, except that I sensed the presence of evil in the room. I began to stare at the upper left-hand corner above my bed and I saw a creature slowly take shape like a storm cloud. It was a monkey, black but glowing around the edges, with venom and filth and slime drooling down his hairy face. He just hung there dribbling and cackling and all the time his phosphorescent eyes were riveted on me. I lay on my back trembling and whimpering. My bones were like water. He hovered there, waiting, his menacing arms waving like poisonous tentacles. I knew that he was concentrated evil, and that all of his emanations were directed at me.

I'm a firm rationalist, but the existence of this thing was never disputable. This wasn't a nightmare or fantasy projection; it was an actual demon filling me with supernatural energy. I tore my mind apart searching for the reason why he was here, but there was no answer. He simply was. My mind was infected as well as my body, there was no escape from his pervasive evil. Finally I got hold of myself enough to say: "Okay, he's here and he's got me, so *what's going to happen?*" And I thought: *He's going to kill me.* Then I remembered that car accidents and falling rocks lead to the same thing, and that death would at least put a stop to this torture. Slowly, slowly, the monkey began to fade and the evil began to neutralize. I ran my hands over my body and found that I was still there. And then he was gone.

Caged monkeys always strike me as degraded animals; slimy and servile and vindictive, all day long imitating humans like mirrors in a madhouse. That's how my monkey was, spewing ugly reflections of myself through his crazy leer. But his appearance marked the first time in my life that I wasn't able to draw a moral from an experience, the first time I accepted the fantastic without any rationale. So now I have a strange feeling of friendliness toward him, a little as if he was a gift from the gods, or a minor foot soldier detached from the army of the Devil to bring me a taste of absolute terror. That monkey devil is permanently seated in my reality. I don't actually think about him much, but I know that sooner or later (what kind of a schedule could he be on?) he'll be back to give me another dose. Wherever he is and whatever evil he embodies, he clearly belongs to me.

A Time and a Place for Everything

My world is full of gods and goddesses, but they aren't the kind that sit on Mount Olympus. They stir among human beings like egg beaters, making waves. They are multitudinous and bodiless, made of color and sound. There is no hierarchy among them, not even a presiding Zeus. All of the gods have influence, but none has the power to rule absolutely. This is a list of the gods I know best:

God of Greed and Selfishness (always provoking, never listening)

God of Pain (inflicts sorrow mechanically, like Sisyphus pushing on his rock, without joy or regret)

Goddess of Healing (shadows Pain to nurse the wounded; dresses in pale green, the color of new shoots)

Goddess of Motherhood (two-faced: one warm, nurturing, caring; the other pinched and possessive)

God of Laughter (young and golden; Pan-like but found in apartments and delicatessens as well as sylvan glades; the genuine, pealing laughter of children)

Gods of Light, Beauty, the Arts (deep colors and clear, high voices)

God of Wisdom (an old, bearded, beautifully lined face; sees and evaluates to reflect truth without judgment)

Goddess of Mediation and Communication (neutral; tries to keep all doors open; probably pearl gray)

I'd like there to be a princely young Apollo or a powerful feminist Diana in my world, but I just don't see it that way. My gods are on an even keel, pushing and pulling to maneuver human beings into their particular power spheres. The lack of hierarchy means lots of commotion. I guess I experience it this way because I find life choices so difficult to make. Since I've always had a wide range of talent and potential, any new force that came along threatened to change my focus. When I was a little girl bandaging my dolls and dreaming of Florence Nightingale, the God of Healing had my allegiance. After that the God of Dance took hold, and later the God of Wisdom, but when my children were born I switched to the Great Maternal Goddess, trying to match her warm, open face. That's pretty much where I am now, raising a family and acting as general mediator between people.

Sometimes I imagine how different my life would be if I allowed a more passionate, less balanced pantheon of gods to exist. But right now, given my priorities, that isn't possible. Maybe in a dozen years when my kids are running on their own steam I'll be free to change the hierarchy and live more radically. For instance, I'd really like to elevate the God of Art above the God of Pain and settle down to the writing I've always wanted to do. It's not that I expect art to make milk and honey suddenly flow from trees, but I do believe that if people developed a greater capacity for experiencing each other there might be more music and light and laughter in the world. But I don't want you to think that I'm beating my wings against the bars of my cage. For now I'm content to let the deities go on stirring evenly around me.

FLYING IN AND OUT OF TIME

When you're high you are up and out, outside yourself, in the world. Elation means cutting loose from your self, connecting with what's out there.

When you're low you are down and in, withdrawn into yourself, away from the world. Depression means stuck on yourself, lost in thought, out of touch.

Consciousness as we usually experience it is separation. The I looks out at other I's and at the world and perceives that it is separate. I am *not* the chair, *not* the dog, *not* the other person. Separation is a neutral fact that may be experienced positively or negatively. Solitude is delicious; alienation is bitter. If one looks at the world through the barred windows of confinement it seems safer to remain in the prison of the self than to risk the strangeness beyond.

The strongest antidotes for alienated self-consciousness are love and hate. Meeting is merging. Loving and hating spring us free from isolation. An I can get lost in a tree, a stone, Bach's "Air for G String," the Brooklyn Bridge, or anything that attracts it.

The conditions for enjoying strange persons and strange things are identical: cease being a spectator and become a participant; disarm; decide to trust. Welcome what is alien and you will not be alone. When we give up our adversary stance, obsession with alienation eases up. We become freer; we lift off as lovers, parts of some encompassing totality. In our hightest moments we are able to fly through time.

Breaking out of the isolation of the self is similar to (perhaps identical with) the mystical union with the divine life. Mystics of all ages have shared a vision of the trustworthiness and unity of life. In this vision the same divine life force animates people, cats, asparagus, germs. Thus communion is a more ultimate fact than alienation. Isolated self-consciousness is bad karma, sin, illusion, or ignorance. All life is a part of the cosmic dance. That's why getting high is a question of transportation, of learning to travel from in to out, from I to we, from self to world.

VIEWPOINTS

Consciousness is always moving. On any day we may travel from extreme isolation to ecstasy. In theory it's easy to go from one extreme to the other: just turn yourself inside out, make contact. In fact, it is tricky. To travel freely in your interior space you need to know how you keep yourself down and how you get high. It may help to chart the daily and yearly elevation changes in your consciousness.

* How, when, and where do you fly? Recall the times you and the world blended like lovers and there was no end to it. What boosts do you use to get high?

* How do you clip your wings, prevent yourself from soaring, depress yourself? Recall your most blue and desperate times. What tricks do you habitually use to heighten your paranoia and increase your isolation?

* Slip inside some ancient accounts of very high and very low states of consciousness, such as those found in the *Tibetan Book of the Dead,* the *Bhagavad Gita,* or Dante's *Divine Comedy,* and see how they fit you.

When Beethoven Sounds Like Toothpaste

No matter how much I like the way my life is, if I do the same things over and over sooner or later I start closing down, spinning in my own grooves. If you take a Beethoven sonata and play it fourteen hundred times, it eventually starts to sound like a toothpaste commercial! It's damn hard to live in stereophonic sound all the time. After a while I slip into a monotone; I start thinking the universe has stopped turning; that *my* thing is *the* thing, and it's a broken record.

Last December that was happening to me so I took a tab of LSD one morning and walked down to the ocean. The beach was cold and gray and nearly deserted. Even though I had it all to myself I staked out a mile or so and set out to inspect my territory. At first I tried to worry about my life but I had been over my troubles so many times that I was bored with them, and anyway my body kept breaking out into movement. Soon I was running and leaping through the fog, cruising on automatic pilot, and anxiety didn't have a chance. I rolled up my pants and played in and out of the waves. A couple of dogs were chasing birds. I'd watched them do the same thing a thousand times before, but this time instead of a one-way pursuit I saw that they had a mutual tag game going! Birds and dogs picked worthy partners and played hilariously. I cheered for a certain bird; then a dog; then another bird, and they all played harder and harder, stimulated by the audience.

After several hours of moving and musing a clear, quiet voice inside my head said, *"The universe is not hostile. Everything around you is all right."* Then I realized that *I* was all right too, exactly as I was, without qualification or future commitments or the benefit of someone else's generosity.

There was nothing I had to do to qualify. (Qualify? For what? For whom?) The water and sand and fog and animals and I were perfectly compatible. I understood that my anxiety didn't have to do with my *existence*, but with the rules and values made up by human beings. A terrible pressure gave way in me as soon as I recalled that the human world isn't everything. . . .

VII

THE END AND
THE BEGINNING

So long as human beings change and make history, so long as children are born and old people die, there will be tales to explain why sorrow darkens the day and stars fill the night. We invent stories about the origin and conclusion of life because we are exiles in the middle of time. The void surrounds us. We live within a parenthesis surrounded by question marks. Our stories and myths don't dispel ignorance, but they help us find our way, our place at the heart of the mystery. In the end, as in the beginning, there will be a vast silence, broken by the sound of one person telling a story to another.

VIEWPOINT

Where did life come from? Where is it going? When will life, the world end? Make up a myth about the creation of the world. About its destiny.

The Joker Is Wild

Once there were two substances, water and earth, which had never touched. They floated timelessly in the darkness. There was neither time nor place nor process, but at the end of infinity water and earth bumped into each other. Water rolled against the land and stayed there, lapping the shore. This licking and tickling continued until one moment the edges of earth felt the motion and giggled. Consciousness was born, laughter was the child of this long relationship. Eventually the water's massage grew so intense that the land mass coughed bubbles of air under the sea, creating animation. Sea creatures, popped from bubbles, crawled onto the land and grew into birds, kangaroos, centipedes, and humans. The apes with the five-fingered hands found fire and claimed it, while explosions of birth and laughter swirled around them in musical spheres. Life multiplied, men and women named each other and made up stories, and death with her long hands took care of everything. But the human creatures who loved to make things fell into the habit of making each other, and soon there were so many feet on the land that laughter was stomped underground, crushed like summer grapes. So the people squeezed the carbonation from their bellies and strained upward, building theologies, skyscrapers, arguments, missiles. Soon they stood heart to heart, pushing and jumping to make room for their own, so that laughter was forced to the very center of the earth. The land bore it until she could hold no longer. Then her great axial bones cracked like glass and bombs of laughter shot forth, opening up the earth. All creatures were swallowed together. Again there was stillness, only water lapping against the land.